*Communication, Knowledge, and
Memory in Early Modern Spain*

Communication, Knowledge, and Memory in Early Modern Spain

FERNANDO BOUZA

Translated by Sonia López and Michael Agnew
FOREWORD BY ROGER CHARTIER

PENN

University of Pennsylvania Press

Philadelphia

Publication of this volume was assisted by a grant from the Program for Cultural Cooperation between Spain's Ministry of Education, Culture and Sports, and United States Universities.

The translation has been made possible through the help of the General Office of Books, Archives, and Libraries of Spain's Ministry of Education, Culture, and Sports.

Originally published as *Comunicación, Conocimiento y Memoria en la España de los Siglos XVI y XVII* by Seminario de Estudios Medievales y Renacentistas, Universidad de Salamanca
Copyright © 1999 Fernando Bouza

10 9 8 7 6 5 4 3 2 1

Published by
University of Pennsylvania Press
Philadelphia, Pennsylvania 19104-4011

Library of Congress Cataloging-in-Publication Data

Bouza Alvarez, Fernando J.
    Communication, knowledge, and memory in early modern Spain / Fernando Bouza : translated by Sonia López and Michael Agnew ; foreword by Roger Chartier.
    [Communicación, conocimiento y memoria en la España de los siglos XVI y XVII. English]
        p.   cm. (Material Texts)
    ISBN 0-8122-3805-2 (cloth : alk. paper)
    Includes bibliographical references and index.
    1. Written communication—Spain—History. I. Title. II. Series.
P211.3.S7 B6813   2004
302.2'244—dc22   2004043546

For Hera K. Olmen
Por más que la miel

Contents

Foreword

ROGER CHARTIER

Communication, Knowledge, and Memory in Early Modern Spain is the first book to appear in English by Fernando Bouza, a scholar whose work over the past twenty years has been enriched by an exceptional knowledge of print production and of the public and private archives of the Spanish Golden Age.

In Sonia López and Michael Agnew's graceful and precise translation, the writing of one of the most inventive of Spanish historians is at last made available to a broader audience of readers. Bouza's goal in this book is an ambitious one: "to outline a history of communication during the Spanish Golden Age that would bring together speech, images, and written texts, presenting them as all serving the same objective: the will to know and to create memory." In this sense, the four chapters of the book offer an extension of the author's two preceding works, which he had consecrated, respectively, to a reflection on the effects of the invention of printing located within the entire framework of written culture and an analysis of the different resources, iconographic and textual, that were mobilized for the construction and diffusion of the figure of the king in the age of Philip II.[1] In each case, his procedure was the same: to frame a view of the whole by offering case studies or textual analyses founded on "first-hand documentary sources."

The greatest originality of the book, now available in English, rests in the connection it makes between two histories too long kept separate: the history of the book and reading on the one side, and the history of the uses of writing on the other. The history of reading practices has traditionally focused on explorations of levels of literacy, as deduced from the numbers of signatures in notarial and parish documents; the uneven penetration of books into different social milieux, as revealed by library inventories, for example; or the diversity of the thematic composition of book collections. The history of the uses of writing has focused on other objects: on the control of written spaces, on the standards and the teaching of writing; on writing's political and administrative uses; and on the publication and production of manuscripts.[2] Bouza's goal is to reconstruct in its totality the "graphic culture" (as Petrucci has called it) of Spain in the early modern period, without drawing artificial boundaries between reading and writing practices.

Bouza certainly recognizes that reading and writing belong to two distinct models of acculturation. The spread of reading literacy is linked to the churches' desire that the faithful interiorize the demands of Christianity through their own reading of the catechism, books of spirituality, devotional works, and, in reformed lands, the Bible itself, translated into the vernacular. The mastery of writing, on the other hand, stems from a desire on the part of individuals or communities who see in the ability to write as a tool useful for the management of daily life or social relations, or even for a possible ascent up the social scale. In most countries in Europe, each skill had its own assigned places and techniques (spelling was taught in primary school, copying in the workshop of the master writer), its own allotted time (the teaching of writing came after the acquisition of the ability to read), and its proper end, whether to subjugate the reader to the authority of texts, and consequently to the institutions that produced and imposed them, or to permit the individual who knew how to write to remove him or herself from the institutions' control and surveillance.[3]

This dichotomy governed the ideology that deemed learning how to read without writing sufficient in popular milieux, and adequate for women. In this context, Bouza cites the canon Pedro Sánchez, who limned the portrait of the ideal woman in his *Arbol de consideración y varia doctrina* (*Tree of Consultation and Varied Teaching*), published in

1548: "It is unnecessary for her to know how to write. . . . She should pray devotedly with a rosary and if she knows how to read, she should read devotional books and books of good doctrine, for writing must be left to men. She should know how to use a needle well and how to use a spindle and distaff, having no need for the use of a pen." Nevertheless, and often with difficulty, at least some humble folk and women appropriated for themselves the ability to write, and breached the boundaries imposed on them by the dominant model. There are many signs of this. First of all, the needle often served as a pen, and embroidery or tapestry was the school or medium for women's writing.[4] Moreover, manuscript documents mentioned by inventories after death or preserved in family archives testify more often than one would expect to the practice of writing in popular contexts. Account books, tallies of debts and payments, family books, personal journals all reveal that the economic necessities of the shop or the workplace carried forward a widely shared desire to write, as did personal aspirations.[5]

In Golden Age Spain, such a mastery of writing would seem to have been advanced by the fact that school masters were contractually required to teach both reading and writing, thus responding to the necessity articulated by Covarrubias in his *Tesoro de la lengua castellana o española* (1611) that "writing has to be taught at the same time as reading to all children." Thus, peasants would be able "not only to plough the soil, but also to make accounts for knowing what they pay and what they receive, and not to make these mentally, scribbling against the wall, which can lead them to make mistakes and be deceived."

But even for those who knew neither how to read nor how to write, the entry into written culture remained possible. Bouza draws up a list of the different realities that permitted "the high degree of familiarity with writing among the illiterate." He underlines, first of all, the ubiquity of writing, in different forms, in early modern cities: shop signs, printed posters, monumental or funerary inscriptions, defamatory placards, graffiti, and so forth. These publicly exposed writings, offered for decipherment to whoever could read them for themselves or for others, seem to have been as numerous in the cities of Spain as they were in Italy or England.[6] From the fifteenth century on, moreover, the activity of booksellers added to the abundance of writings already to be found stuck to walls or carved in stone, with the circulation of printed texts destined for the most numerous and least lettered of readers. The *pliegos sueltos* (chap books), sold and sometimes composed by blind peddlers who controlled their distribution, offered to common readers (and listeners) *romances, coplas,* and *relaciones de sucesos*—that is to say, printed materials either taking up the matter or form of oral poetry, or offering accounts in prose of extraordinary happenings.[7] There, once again, the Spanish world knew an editorial formula that had its equivalents, perhaps a bit later, in the broadside ballads and chapbooks of England and the *Bibliothèque bleue* of France.[8]

In these two cases of exposed writing on walls and peddlers' pamphlets, Bouza indicates that the possible circulation of texts extended well beyond the population of men and women who were able to read them. Reading aloud was a frequent practice which assured the sharing of texts beyond the cohort of the literate.[9] It is important not to limit the practice of reading aloud to popular settings, for it was, as well, very much a habit of literate and aristocratic sociability. Its use persisted as an ecclesiastical instrument for controlling the proper interpretation of texts by their auditors. Nevertheless, reading aloud remained the means throughout Europe by which the most humble members of society could enter into the culture of the written word. Bouza's analysis, then, does not surprise when he underlines that "writing became a principal characteristic of early modern civilization," and he devotes the two final chapters of his book to the "significant stamp that writing left on Spanish culture in the sixteenth and seventeenth centuries." Writing became the instrument for the governance of places and people; literate knowledge was founded on books and reading; and in the cities, at least, the culture shared by most of the population was deeply penetrated by a familiarity with the numerous texts to be read on walls, purchased from the blind, heard, and shared.

Any such summary is a serious betrayal of Fernando Bouza's book, however. The realities that he describes and analyzes are much more complex. First, and resisting the powerful temptation offered by the work of Elizabeth Eisenstein,[10] he shows that one cannot simply understand print culture to have vanquished scribal culture in the sixteenth and seventeenth centuries. During the Golden Age, the discourse of mistrust or scorn for printing proliferated; somber diagnoses of the dangers of the increase in numbers of useless books, the corruption of texts by clumsy typesetters and ignorant readers, the bad manners of booksellers and printers abounded.[11] Meanwhile, the increased production of printed materials in no way marked the disappearance of the multiple uses of manuscript. Sketching out matters he has developed more fully elsewhere,[12] Bouza here inventories the multiple functions assigned to handwritten documents in the age of printing. As in England during this period,[13] a manuscript copy could assure publication of numerous kinds of works: political satires, poetic collections, heterodox texts. More readily than typographic composition, manuscript permitted reproduction of copies of archival documents and even printed books in a limited number. It preserved the secrecy and flexibility of texts not meant to fall into the hands of the public, or of those, such as the instructions nobles compiled for the instruction of their sons, which were subject to constant addition.

Above all, manuscript composition constituted the essential instrument for the intellectual technique of the commonplace which, in literate settings, governed both reading and writing.[14] The practice presupposes that the reader, whether student or scholar, mark in the margins of printed books those passages which are to be remembered, that he copy them into a memo- or notebook, and that he then make a fair copy of them in a commonplace book organized by themes and topics. What is involved here is the construction of a true library of extracts, examples, and references, available for the composition of new discourses, including literary ones, which require the *copia verborum ac rerum*, which are constructed from variations on borrowed themes or motifs, and which presuppose the accumulation of references to *auctoritates*. Such a technique was common to all people of erudition in Renaissance Europe, and it provided the initiative to publishers who facilitated the work of readers by offering them ready-made collections of printed commonplace books.[15] It is one of Fernando Bouza's significant contributions to demonstrate, on the basis of the *notata*, or collections of extracts assembled by Spanish readers, that the Iberian peninsula shared in the practices of the most dynamic strongholds of Humanism.

The verdict is, then, clear: printing did not cause the manuscript to disappear, and the manuscript remained a fundamental instrument for the composition, transmission, and publication of texts in the early modern period. But that is not the most important point for Bouza.

His essential thesis consists, in effect, in the affirmation that the progress of textual culture, in all its forms, in no way lessened the importance granted in the sixteenth and seventeenth centuries to two other mediums of knowledge, memory, and persuasion: that is, the image and oral discourse. In the very original analysis that opens the book, Bouza shows how the three modes of communication—the living word, the painted or engraved image, and the written or printed text—were considered equivalent forms of knowledge, accorded an equal capacity for signifying "the thing and the concept itself," as the Portuguese Diego Henrique de Vilhegas had written in 1692 in his book, *Leer sin libro* (*Reading Without a Book*).

The fact of such an equivalence has many consequences. On the one hand, it allows for a choice from one or another of the available languages, based not on the nature of the message to be transmitted, but on the imagined audience and the circumstances of communication. Moreover, the equivalence establishes the use of the three mediums of expression in every social setting, from the most humble to the most aristocratic.[16] Firmly rejecting an opposition between popular and literary culture that is too readily accepted by historians, Bouza shows that orality is as strongly present in the world of the court as in popular settings, that the image can be put to all kinds of uses, from the most learned to the most naïve, and that, as one has seen, writing is not simply the privilege of the powerful, but something that touches even the illiterate. In this sense, his book is an important contribution to the reevaluation of cultural differentiation in the societies of the ancien régime, and deserves a place alongside all those works which have brought attention to the fluidity of the circulation of texts, images, and ideas among the different levels of a single society.[17]

By stressing the equivalence between orality, the image, and the written text, Bouza is not arguing that individuals of the sixteenth and seventeenth centuries ignored the specificity of each. Thus the performative force of the word to curse, conjure, or convince; the capacity of the visual image to give presence to the absent being or thing; or the possibility of the reproduction and preservation of texts which only writing, and more particularly printing, makes imaginable. It is this awareness of the differences that justifies the simultaneous use of the three modes of communication, for example in the genre of the emblem or the practice of preaching. At the same time, the difference affords the possibility for the movement of a single "discourse" from one mode into another, as for example, with the myth of the survival of the Portuguese king Sebastian, which moves first from rumor into pictures, and then into print narrative.[18]

The ambivalent judgment that recognizes, at once, the equality of the different forms of communication and their specific capacities legitimizes both the complementarity of their uses and the efforts made to capture in each the effects proper to the other two. It is the case, when some printed genres attempt to seize or imitate the formulas of orality, that printed editions of proclamations, sermons, or theatrical plays strive to restore something of the living word, or that catechisms, pamphlets, or treatises on natural philosophy mobilize the resources of dialogue.[19] Counter to the idea, inherited from the nineteenth century, of a radical difference between the written word and other forms of communication, Fernando Bouza underlines the strong and durable presence of the powers of the image and the voice in writing: "images and speech . . . remained present also in that specific realization of writing which is reading. Writing continued to maintain a lively and intense relationship with those other two forms of communication, knowledge, and memory, perhaps because in writing, too, there resided something of that essential creativity which we have seen manifested in a voice that upbraids or blesses and in the powerful images whose contemplation was propitiatory."

Such an observation allows us not just to resist the temptation of the anachronism that protects writing from all contamination by the forms of communication it is supposed to have marginalized. It also opens the way for new research, for example, into studies inventorying those writings which have a performative force identical to certain oral pronouncements, or analyses such as Bouza himself has made in his book *Imagen y propaganda*, which pinpoint the exchanges between images constructed as discourse and writings invested with the visual power of the ekphrasis. Returning to the pioneering reflections of Louis Marin, Bouza thus underlines the complexity of the relationship between text and image in a time when—as emblems demonstrate—they were thought of as two languages using the same grammar, if not the same lexicon, all the while being granted their own specific powers, thus justifying their juxtaposition, imbrications, or exchanges.[20]

Fernando Bouza refuses to accept the simplifications, received ideas, and myths which have deeded to us a history inclined to identify rationality and modernity with written culture only, relegating to the past or the popular the language of images and the practices of orality. This book (like all the others he has written, and which one hopes will also be translated) offers testimony to the great talent of a historian who is erudite, rigorous, and imaginative. Beyond that, it illustrates the vitality of an entire generation of Spanish historians who are too little known and read beyond the international community of Hispanists. Over the course of the past twenty years, Spanish scholars have proposed an original intersection of cultural history and textual criticism. The encounter has produced noteworthy work in a number of different fields: the history of publishing, the history of the practices of writing and reading, the history of censorship.[21] A community has emerged in Spain that is fully open to the reception of foreign scholarship. It would be both just and useful if the contrary were true today, and if the original methodological and theoretical propositions elaborated for understanding the historical realities of the Iberian peninsula were more widely known and applied to other historical situations. There is no better demonstration of the necessity for this than this elegant and acutely intelligent book by Fernando Bouza.

Translated by Jerome Singerman

Communication, Knowledge, and Memory in Early Modern Spain

Hearing, Seeing, Reading, and Writing: The Forms and Uses of Words, Images, and Writing

"The cruelty with which time consumes everything is fierce, for neither strong armor nor iron walls can sustain its blows."[1] This sentence—halfway between heartfelt lament and dry proverb—was uttered before a portrait of Prince Philibert of Savoy, which, lacking any identifying inscription, seemed now almost beyond recognition. The scene appears in an account of the visit by a group of gentlemen to the typical gallery of illustrious men expected of every noble seventeenth-century household. The account concludes with a *letrilla* (a poem of short verses and a brief refrain) in which a former servant of the Prince, the only person able still to recognize him, proposes to save his former master from unjust oblivion with "a sword made from a goose's plume / and bolstered by a paper shield."[2]

Pen and paper are the arms of the writer; though flimsy objects, they are powerful in their own way. That writing can triumph over time by compensating for its cruel effects is one of the arguments typically proffered in defense of the written word in the sixteenth and seventeenth centuries. Thus, in 1602, the Augustinian friar Pedro de Vega proclaims roundly in his *Segunda parte de la declaración de los siete salmos penitenciales* (*Second Part of the Declaration of the Seven Penitential Psalms*) that writing "was invented to support and restore our memory."[3] Memory must also have been an original motive for reading, since, as Friar Pedro adds, "one's memory only gains strength when one reads again and again that which was already beginning to fade into oblivion."[4]

To forge a memory of things, ideas, and people through the transmission of knowledge of their deeds, sentiments, and passions was one of the main objectives of writing in the sixteenth and seventeenth centuries. Of course, as Yates has shown, memory was then something more than mere mnemonics, more than a simple artifice for the purpose of recollection; on the contrary, memory was raised to the category of a true art that enabled one's own access to knowledge and permitted its transmission to others. It goes without saying that at that time people took for granted the existence of other ways of knowing, such as divine revelation, prophecies (expressed often in dreams), inspiration, and, of course, divination. In contrast to these sources of knowledge, however, only memory would have been seen as characteristically human, joined by reason and the senses.

Few matters provoked more interest in the early modern period than memory, because it is an essential aspect of the human condition. Thus, in the same way that oblivion was understood to be the inescapable consequence of human frailty (on a par, therefore, with death), the possibility of creating memory offered a potentially perfect manifestation of the extraordinary natural capacities of humankind.

Among the numerous gifts supposedly granted to human beings by God (who presumably exists without memory, since eternity is his present) was the ability to invent, by means of reason and ingenuity, some way of defeating the oblivion to which humans' own mortal nature condemned them. Writing thus seemed to be a subtle artifice sprung from human inventiveness, an expression of man's status as *homo faber*, that is, as artful builder. Therefore, in the typically early modern praise of things human—with which so many authors occupied themselves throughout the sixteenth and seventeenth centuries—there usually appear references to writing as that with which one could attempt to defeat time.

In this regard, let us briefly consider European intellectuals' discussion of cultures without writing, such as certain Native American peoples. For instance, in his *Histórica relación del Reyno de Chile* (*Historical Account of the Kingdom of Chile*), Father Alonso de Ovalle came to wonder how Andean peoples, unaware of writing until the arrival of Europeans, managed to preserve memory. The Jesuit did not doubt that, despite their illiteracy, they could by oral means preserve for posterity a kind of memory embodied in a certain individual whom he describes as the "archive of that people," and whose obligatory function consisted of "every holy day repeating to the rhythm of a drum the story of events since the flood, singing according to the customs of that place, in order to keep that memory within him. To make certain this memory would never fade, he was required to instruct others who would follow him in this office after his death."[5] In short, where there was humanity, there was memory.

As I have indicated, writing was not considered the sole expression of humans' essential capacity to create memory. The same power was attributed to painted or sculpted images and to the spoken word, forms of expression about which their many defenders were more than ready to affirm that, being perceived by eyes or ears, they could also serve memory as effectively and persuasively as necessary. Thus, for instance, the alluded-to portrait galleries of famous men so common in the age of the Renaissance and the Baroque only take on their fullest significance when viewed as museums of Fame in which the moral virtues of the depicted heroes could be clearly discerned by merely beholding their painted images. In turn, from the standpoint of orality, the rich tradition of famous courtiers' sayings and maxims transmitted at first only orally, for the enjoyment of their contemporaries and later for the instruction of their descendants, contributed to a form of memory associated particularly with aristocratic courts—not to mention the malicious rumors and defamatory criticisms, also divulged and preserved by principally oral means, aimed at condemning a person's memory and whose abundance was such that at least one writer has defined early modern Europe as a society of derision.

Thus, one could claim that reading, writing, seeing, and hearing waged a kind of battle on memory's behalf in the sixteenth and seventeenth centuries. That former servant of the Prince of Savoy must have been referring to this hypothetical battle, in which voices, images, and texts intervene, when, brandishing his pen and paper in the face of the insufficiencies of portraiture and the silence of oral fame, for the sake of preserving the prince's memory, he promised,

A sword made from a goose's plume
and bolstered by a paper shield
against time's cruelty I shall wield,
lest of his exploits it consume
one tittle on Fame's battlefield.[6]

The reconstruction of that rich, long, and fascinating debate between reading, writing, seeing, and hearing in the sixteenth and seventeenth centuries represents the main objective of the following pages, intended not so much to analyze the ideas forged, deliberated, divulged, or rejected in Hapsburg Spain, as to explain how such ideas were expressed, the formal means by which people thought these ideas could be conveyed, and how and why they were used in both learned and popular culture according to the respective needs of each.

Regarding the necessities that speech, images, or texts fulfilled, each in its own way, it is to be recalled that in the Renaissance and Baroque age a particular ideal of social control with its attendant pedagogical elements had developed, aimed at guiding a person's conduct. I suggested above that memory was essentially human; in that period, human beings could also be defined by their capacity to learn.

Thus, in his *Arte para conocernos a nosotros mismos por señales exteriores* (*Art of Knowing Ourselves by Our Outward Appearance*), Friar Alvaro Cavide proclaims in a chapter entitled, "Como sólo el hombre es diçiplinable" ("How Only Man Is Subject to Schooling"), that since only humans are capable of learning, "man alone studies and learns and by his very nature wishes to know more."[7] The corollary to this definition of humanity is, of course, that it is possible to teach or discipline humans, and consequently the most practical means of doing so should be sought out. From the standpoint of early modern communicative practices, impelled and sustained by the desire to guide behavior, the use of speech, images, or texts depended upon their capacity to convince or persuade, or at best to persuade convincingly or convince persuasively.

In short, my approach has relatively little to do with the theoretical exposition of the principles of rationality and perception but rather explores the practical field of social customs and forms closely related to memory—in the terms proposed by Yates—and the requirements of social discipline, understood as pedagogy or propaganda. I should add that such a reconstruction of contemporary polemic over these matters is possible based on testimonies from the period (which are fortunately quite numerous) perhaps because at their root one can glimpse more profound arguments about the scope of human inventiveness and artifice.

Of course, one should not forget that the debate I will attempt to portray here will end up leaning gradually in favor of writing until the nineteenth-century apotheosis of graphophilia, when a seemingly inseparable link between writing and rationality was definitively drawn—in other words, a link between writing and progress. In addition, artists in the nineteenth century assert the self-sufficiency of the images they create, legitimated by the notion of artistic freedom, not by the obligation to serve as instruments of pedagogy or propaganda. Meanwhile, the autonomy of oral expression as a form of communication, knowledge, and memory will decline considerably in the face of increased literacy and growing industrialization.

Nonetheless, the insistence among historians on writing as a defining feature of modernity should also be considered in relation to the notable advances in the general introduction of writing after the invention of the printing press in the mid-fifteenth century. However, this indisputable fact, which historians must necessarily give an account of, became colored by certain prejudices connected less to the concrete reality of communication in the sixteenth and seventeenth centuries than to views about the role of history in the nineteenth century and much of the twentieth.

As is well known, contemporary historiography has long been dominated—very much at its core—by an anachronistic prejudice, which transformed the sixteenth and seventeenth centuries into the initial stage of modernization, a prelude anticipating and preparing the ground for our own contemporary age. Thus, the role of historians has been to explain their own concurrent realities, endowing them with a certain logic—from the modern state to industrial production, including, along the way, the bourgeois family, the individual subject, and, of course, science and the intellect.

In the concrete field of the history of communication, this implied focusing on the emergence or consolidation of contemporary forms of reading and writing, upon the foundation of the presumed link I have already mentioned between the conceptual destinies of writing and rationality, joined in the processes of modernization and progress. Modernity became associated exclusively with writing conceived as a rational activity, and, consequently, instances of oral and visual culture after the appearance of the printing press came to be viewed as forms of expression that, though quite possibly beautiful in their own right, were always somehow antiquated, manifesting hardly innovative values.

In this way, while writing, especially typography, became identified with the arrival and continuance of the early modern period, oral and visual culture were reduced to vestiges of the Middle Ages, a stereotype that still enjoys some favor among the general public. Therefore, writing the history of communication in the early modern period amounted fundamentally to tracing the "progress" of reading and writing from the fifteenth to the eighteenth centuries. Needless to say, in practice, what mattered was not so much to learn how people obtained knowledge—or believed one could obtain knowledge—in 1550 or 1600, but rather to determine what had happened then such that in 1850 or 1900 writing had become the basis for knowledge in the West.

As I have already pointed out, one cannot deny the evident advances made by writing after the fifteenth century thanks as much to the invention of typography—the new *ars artificialiter scribendi* (art of writing artificially)—as to the gradual, definitive implantation of the written report in different governmental agencies' communications with the king and of other types of written documents in the task of governance. This does not mean, however, that one must accept the double corollary some have attempted to derive from the extraordinary role of writing in the formation of modern European civilization: first, that as a form of communication, visual images came to be viewed as essentially contrary to written texts—a dichotomy arbitrarily extended to the crucial areas of religious and political conflict (the Reformation and the new political regime being to writing as the Counter-Reformation and the ancien régime are to visual culture); and second, that orality, likewise opposed to writing, came to define the realm of the popular, thus erasing all traces it might have left in early modern learned or courtly culture, which as a consequence became completely dependent upon writing, losing their former oral dimension.

Nevertheless, in the sixteenth and seventeenth centuries no one seems to have doubted that images or speech alone could convey any concept, regardless of its complexity, rivaling in expressiveness even writing—that eventually omnipresent, apparently omnipotent form of communication. Before considering the possible powers accorded to speech, images and written characters in the early modern period, let me first introduce that "master of first letters," Blas Antonio de Ceballos, and a most singular work of his, in which he presents writing in its relationship to images and spoken words in very different terms than was reconceived by the nineteenth century. That work is the *Libro histórico y moral sobre el origen y excelencias del nobilíssimo arte de leer, escribir y contar y su enseñanza* (*Historical and Moral Book Regarding the Origin and Excellences of the Most Noble Art of Reading, Writing and Narrating and Its Teaching*), printed in Madrid in 1692, one of the first histories of the teaching of reading and writing in Europe and to which I will have occasion to return later, in Chapter 4.

For the moment, however, it is pertinent to highlight a circumstance related to this author's particular perspective (a matter significant for the proper understanding of any cultural phenomenon from the past). In 1692, Ceballos drafted his encomiastic history of the *nobilíssimo arte* of reading and writing and their instruction in printed books, at the same time that he was perpetuating that very tradition (now 150 years old) in his own noble professional capacity as an active teacher and calligrapher and author of such a book. In other words, his perspective is twofold, bringing together both that of the chronicler who has left us a well documented source and that of a person who is part of the very history he narrates, in this case, the history of the teaching of reading and writing in Spain from the reign of Emperor Charles V (King Charles I of Spain 1517–1556), to that of Charles II (1661–1700).

This circumstance, hardly insignificant, lends extraordinary value to Ceballos's book, given recent historians' aim to understand past cultural phenomena in their own conceptual context, freeing historical analysis from anachronism as much as possible. In this sense, Ceballos's *Historical and Moral Book* is also a theoretical text that allows us to see the position he adopts as a polemicist in the alluded-to debate over the parameters of writing and its relationship to images and the spoken word. Let us examine, for instance, the terms in which he presents the invention of that special class of correspondence between relatives and friends, which at that time was typically called "familiar correspondence."

According to Ceballos, the existence of this kind of written document dated back to remotest antiquity, to the age of the legendary

Iberian king Túbal, who in a stroke of genius invented such missives "to learn of the doings of relatives and friends dwelling in other provinces."[8] He continues: "These were the first form of correspondence used in the world. Properly considered, they are a private conversation, an instrument through which to reveal the intimate thoughts of one's heart, and the pen becomes a sixth sense for those who are absent or a breath that inspires the soul in the same way a portrait delights one's gaze."[9] Thus, Master Ceballos asserted in 1692 that writing could be considered a form of conversation, that is, a substitute for orality that makes it possible for those absent to understand the writer's ideas and feelings, equating pen and paintbrush, both of which give life to something inert in communicating what they portray.

In contradistinction to this early modern view of writing as a reflection of an absent image or echo of an absent voice, according to which writing is understood as a faithful copy of that which is oral or visual, more recent histories of communication in the early modern period, as I have indicated, have long been dominated by what one might call the tyrannical empire of writing. They consequently disregard visual or oral knowledge as somehow backward. This passage from Ceballos, however, reveals rather the idea that writing sought to imitate speech and images, and his case is not unique. Pedro de Navarra Labrit, for example, offers an extraordinary definition of writing in his *Diálogos de la differencia del hablar al escrivir* (*Dialogues on the Difference Between Speaking and Writing*, 1565): it is "a portrait that captures the moment of speech or the glorious rumor of the words that is left after you have spoken; a likeness or reanimated life, which, as soon as you see it, will recall to memory that which it represents, like the painter who paints the portrait of one who is easily recognizable in it."[10] Or, as another example, Lope de Vega, in correspondence with the duke of Sessa, indicates, "I do not know who claimed that letters are a mental speech to those absent, but he spoke rightly, for, as one writes, one is thinking of the person to whom one is writing and speaks with him in one's mind, where his image is represented as if alive."[11]

To the consternation of some nineteenth-century historians, in the sixteenth and seventeenth centuries, a period of abundant praise for writing, there was also ample room for those who mistrusted the written word and even doubted the utility of the printing press, held by the nineteenth century to be so great an instrument of modernization. Let us consider, for instance, the dialogue between the student Leonelo and the peasant Barrildo that concludes the second scene of the second act of Lope de Vega's *Fuente Ovejuna*.

The image of Salamanca that Lope places in the mouth of Leonelo, recently returned from that Castilian city's university to rural Fuente Obejuna, in the southern province of Cordova, is that of urban streets and squares full of signs and placards. Undoubtedly, Leonelo's portrayal of the city is hardly intended to be generous, for the new licenciate assures Barrildo that in Salamanca "although one might be highly skilled at reading, / he'll find that placard Babel quite misleading."[12] After Lope thus cleverly draws our attention to the increased presence of writing even in city streets, he goes on clearly to praise Johannes Gutenberg, "a man from Mainz whose fame is so complete / that Fame herself with him cannot compete,"[13] and yet he discredits Gutenberg's invention because it has generated such an excess of books that it has become more a source of confusion than of enlightenment. In conclusion, Leonelo pronounces regarding the printing press that

without it many centuries went by,
and now, though blessed with it, our age has seen
no Saint Jerome reborn nor Augustine.[14]

Lope de Vega was not the only one to question the benefits typography had brought in its 150-year history, nor was he the harshest critic. At the beginning of the seventeenth century, the jurist Joan de Orellana would blame the printing press in his *Juiçio de las leyes civiles* (*Judgment on Civil Law*) for the "superfluity and excessive number" of legal texts in circulation.[15] He proposes "denying completely any license to compose books on this subject and preventing the continued admission of such books from abroad, both those already written and those that might be written in the future."[16] The Jesuit António Vieira remarked more wittily that "even Christ refused to allow paper and ink at his execution so that he would not have to pay the legal fees," and, turning to his own century, aptly proclaimed, "now, oh world, you are even more covered in paper, but you are not therefore any the wiser."[17]

Such declarations would surely have annoyed historians in the nineteenth-century tradition had they paid attention to this sort of testimony. Undoubtedly they would have condemned as indicative of an antiquated mentality such allegations about typography's disreputability made by those who in the sixteenth and seventeenth centuries perceived it as writing's "dark side." Nevertheless, the combined evidence for the existence in Spain and abroad of what has been characterized by Rodríguez de la Flor as early modern "biblioclasm" is so noteworthy that one cannot simply cast aside such critical attitudes as symptomatic of obscurantism—attitudes that, regarding the virtues of printed books in particular, were at best suspicious. On the contrary, "biblioclasm" clearly constitutes another aspect of the history of the modern book that must be taken into account and that can only be explained from the standpoint of older notions about writing.

While Blas Antonio de Ceballos presented writing in 1692 as a copy of spoken conversation and a surrogate for painted representations of living beings, the Portuguese writer Diogo Henriques de Vilhegas had theorized twenty years before about how words, images, and texts convey knowledge in his invaluable *Leer sin libro: Direcciones acertadas para el govierno éthico, económico y político* (*Reading Without a Book: Sound Instructions for Ethical, Efficient, and Shrewd Government*). Though his work contains not a single engraving, "Captain Villegas" (as the Castilians called this man who had served for many years in the armies of Philip IV) proposes a peculiar pedagogical system based on symbolic readings of trees and plants, a veritable fount of exempla for that man who must govern his community, his family, and himself. Before proposing, however, his pedagogical botany (a kind of αντο-/αυτοσοφία), Vilhegas analyzes with great precision the nature of images and how they can become examples for human behavior. At the same time, he explains why reading and speech allow one to obtain knowledge.

Thus, he indicates that speech, images, and written characters allow one to signify "the thing or the concept itself," although "speech or words" are only good for "communicating concepts of the mind to those who are present," while we can resort to "written characters— letters or images—for the purpose of declaring our plans, thoughts and feelings to those who are absent, or to make ourselves known to a third party."[18] Another aspect of Vilhegas's approach is worth noting, one which again would contradict well-established nineteenth-century stereotypes, namely, the intimate connection it establishes between images and written texts by considering both an image and a letter as a kind of character. On the contrary, the stereotype would seek to separate writing from images, making the latter parallel to speech as manifestations of "premodern" or "antimodern" culture. But Captain Vilhegas nonetheless insists that "reading is a form of perception," and "looking at an image leads it directly to the intellect itself."[19]

In short, in the sixteenth and seventeenth centuries there already existed a clear awareness that what was oral, visual/iconic, and written (manifested as printed and manuscript texts and as public or silent reading) all fulfilled the same expressive, communicative, and recollective functions. One must add the proviso, of course, that images and written characters could present knowledge not just once, but repeatedly, because of their relative permanence. In other words, images and texts are useful for dissemination, while direct speech, thought to be more "genuine," allowed for more immediate communication of precise knowledge in its transitoriness.

Though I have affirmed the basic equivalence of the three persons of this communicative trinity (oral, visual, and written expression), it is important nonetheless to emphasize that they were employed differently in different circumstances, whether individually or in conjunction. (Emblems, for example, combine text and image; a sermon combines oral and visual/iconic elements in addition to the possibility of becoming a written text.) Of course, it is important to remember that this threefold choice would only be feasible for the literate, since the illiterate, who constituted the bulk of the population, could only have recourse to speech and images to express themselves on their own, although, as we shall see, they came into increasing contact with writing and enjoyed greater access to the medium.

Having made this qualification, I should point out that the ultimate choice of one form of expression or another seems to have depended not on the content of the message, but on the specific needs of the circumstances. (In other words, one cannot maintain simplistically that visual images served only as a traditional medium and a vehicle for that which was orthodox while writing was the ally of innovation or revolution.) The two basic criteria that determined the convenience of one form over another were what we might call the principle of expressivity and the principle of preservation. According to circumstances, one considered speech, images, and manuscripts or printed texts for their expressiveness in practical terms and their capacity to convey truth or its appearance; second, one considered which medium would be more lasting and could guarantee wider dissemination.

Taking into account these basic premises, it is possible to understand the different ways oral, visual, and written texts (print or manuscript) were used. Thus, for example, the ability of print to divulge information was clear, given the availability of numerous inexpensive copies, recommending its usefulness for propaganda. At the same time, however, compared with the autograph manuscript (for example, in correspondence), printed material was presumed to be in a certain sense fraudulent or less truthful because of its status as a commodity marketed for mass consumption. In the polemics, therefore, that matched the propaganda machines of different European powers against each other in the seventeenth century, pamphlets were produced alleging they were faithful copies of, for example, a (fictitious) handwritten letter found by chance—or other such fabrications that would make the product of printing presses seem veracious.

As a second example, one could cite missionaries' work as an activity that relied primarily on oral and visual/iconic communication. Writing could enter into the equation, though only in the form of public readings, since the majority of preachers' audiences were illiterate, and unmediated written texts, printed or handwritten, proved completely useless. Though we still do not know very much about missionary techniques in early modern Spain, it is clear that in order to carry out their pastoral charge, preachers had to adopt what we might call a communicative strategy. Thus, in 1593, the bishop of Calahorra advised, regarding Jesuit missions to the mountainous parts of Basque estates, that "if [the fathers] are not Basque, in no way will they be suitable for the teaching of the faith, for almost none of the inhabitants understands the Romance vernacular, speaking only Basque."[20] Even without the need to overcome such linguistic obstacles, those who proselytized were quite attentive to the conditions of reception of their addressees.

On the one hand, the relationship between preaching and images or paintings in holy places is well documented because it was habitual to draw parallels between verbal imagery in sermons and the scenes represented in churches or in the paintings that preachers could suddenly reveal to the audience in the course of their sermon. This constituted what the Jesuit Jerónimo López called an "industria de espectáculos" ("ingenuity of spectacles," *industria* being translatable for our purposes here also as "strategy").[21] In the missionaries' treatise by Miguel Angel Pascual titled *Oyente preservado y fortalecido* (*The Hearer Saved and Strengthened*), references to the exact moment when the images should be revealed in a sermon appear in the margins to the homiletic texts like theatrical cues, such as, "pull out little by little the portrait of the condemned soul" or "move the portrait closer and pull out the image of Christ."[22]

It is in the biography of Father López by Martín de la Naja titled *El missionero perfecto* (*The Perfect Missionary*), however, that one finds some of these spectacles expounded upon in greater detail: crucifixes, images of the Christ of Sorrows, skulls of the dead, or "portraits" of souls in danger of damnation or already condemned, all of which the Jesuit used in his lengthy missions to Valencia, Catalonia, Aragon, Navarre, and Castile. De la Naja also gives an account of the excesses committed by some preachers who appeared in the pulpit with a skull in each hand, brandished swords, or had trumpets play behind them, reaching such an extreme that one preacher "for the Easter Sermon hired some loutish errand-boy and showed him to the people half naked and spattered with red ochre, instead of an image of the Man of Sorrows."[23]

Ecclesiastics did not, however, resort only to images, though admittedly they were more prudent than this last preacher, who ended up being reprimanded by the Inquisition. In missionary work within Spain, preachers did not neglect to use the *industria* of oral traditions of learning and transmission of knowledge. Upon returning from New Spain, Bishop Juan Palafox wrote his *Bocados espirituales, políticos, místicos y morales* (*Spiritual, Political, Mystic, and Moral Morsels*), in reality a "catechism and compilation of doctrinal axioms for peasants and simple folk."[24] It was intended for parish priests and missionaries working in the diocese of Osma. One of these "morsels" promoted respect for kings and laws by encouraging peasants to learn these simple verses:

Your kings you must respect; their laws do not neglect,
For our republic's lost just when this line is crossed:
All things when poorly tuned, by discord are consumed.
And if the monarch's hated, the monarchy's ill-fated,
Or if he's not obeyed, the kingdom comes unmade.
If magistrates aren't heeded, the people's soon defeated.[25]

Without going into the very particular nature of the subject matter the rural clergy were compelled to teach, it is worth noting that Bishop Palafox seems to be fully aware of the specific conditions of the transmission of knowledge in the rural world by offering these simple, rhymed couplets, which the illiterate could easily memorize, being accustomed to this form of oral transmission. Moreover, scholars have stressed that the successes of the Catholic missionaries in rural seventeenth-century Europe, compared to the failures of Calvinists, was due in a large part to their skill at linking their methods of indoctrination to local traditions and to a fundamentally oral and visual culture, rather than stressing writing as their rivals did.

In fact, the sixteenth and seventeenth centuries witnessed constant reliance on all three forms of communication in close connection, without prejudice regarding their respective efficacy, since, in one form or another they clearly managed to express ideas and emotions. Trembling hands, clouded eyes, tied tongues, and even pens strangely suspended "con arcano sentimiento" ("with mute sentiment") would have been the immediate effects observed with the news of Philip's IV death in 1665, according to the grandiloquent rhetoric of Friar Juan de Santa María in his *Dichoso fin a la vida humana y feliz tránsito a la eterna* (*Fortunate End to Human Life and Happy Passage to Eternity*), the detailed account of the monarch's final moments, published by his former confessor in 1667. Just as the "espanto del alma" ("fright to the soul") that the news provoked at court could be noted in the suspension of speech and sight or even of writing implements, voices, images, and texts also frequently joined to express happier sentiments.

Let us consider, for example, how the belief spread that Sebastian I of Avis did not die in the battle of Alcazarquivir in 1578, and that, therefore, Philip II and his heirs had occupied the Portuguese throne illegitimately. According to a *memorial* (report) written by Diogo Soares around 1644, the news spread at first as a mere rumor— through "idle chat" ("plática") as he calls it—based on the testimony of witnesses who claimed that the king had not died because a generous knight had occupied his place; soon thereafter, "paintings of the event were commissioned."[26] Soares's *Memorial* continues, "These paintings about what was at first a rumor served as new tongues and mute witnesses,"[27] reaffirming the truthfulness of the story, which, last but not least, profited from the possibilities offered by writing when various authors sent their versions to the printing press. In this way, casual conversation, paintings, and texts could maintain and disseminate the idea that Sebastian still lived, an opinion undeniably widespread in Portugal after 1580 and shared by the literate and illiterate alike to the point that it became a general form of resistance against the Spanish Hapsburgs.

That written, iconographic, and oral codes could be considered equally legitimate means of communication, used according to the necessities of circumstance rather than according to a preconceived hierarchy, allows us, furthermore, to reconstruct an arena of cultural dissemination in which the culture of the literate came into contact with that of the illiterate. We can thus overcome a traditional dichotomy in histories of the early modern period that completely closed off the realm of writing from that of oral and visual culture. On the contrary, phenomena such as oral readings help explain the way literate culture could reach the unlettered masses.

In conclusion, during the sixteenth and seventeenth centuries, hearing, seeing, and reading and writing were viewed as three perfectly valid ways to obtain and disseminate knowledge, without presupposing any necessary link between the content of a message and its forms. In practice, what would determine the recourse to speech, images, or texts had to do with specific needs and with the particular capacity to communicate or to preserve knowledge attributed to each. The surviving evidence of practical manifestations of this trio of communicative and recollective resources also helps us better understand the relationship in Hapsburg Spain between lettered and unlettered culture, which, far from being isolated from each other, were in constant and mutually enriching contact. But what exactly was there in a voice, an image or a written text?

Chapter 2

The Persuasion of the Word: A Voice; The Wonder of Images: A Portrait; The Power of Writing: A Talisman

Though it constitutes an immense field of possible research, oral culture remains a challenge that cultural historians of the Spanish Golden Age have hardly confronted. It is true that considerable progress has been made in the linguistic history of the period (vis-à-vis phonetics, morphology, and so forth), in the analysis of so-called oral literature (lyric poetry, exemplary tales, short popular narratives, and so forth) or in the study of rhetoric, given that this was certainly an age of eloquence; our knowledge, however, about the contemporary cultural parameters of the spoken word is scant. Obviously there is an insuperable problem with our sources, since no truly oral text survives. Nonetheless, it is necessary to attempt some systematic approach to what the spoken word represented in sixteenth- and seventeenth-century Spain, a culture of liturgical prayers, town criers, hymns, and formal hearings.

Let us begin with the human voice simply as sound. The first thing of note is the truly astonishing richness of the lexicon applied to different qualities of voice. Sources refer to voices that are clear, raspy, gentle, trembling, melodious, flowing, rustic, sing-song, sonorous, sad, sharp-toned, grave, penetrating, strong, mellifluous, soft, and a long etcetera of timbres, tones, and sonorities that are proof of the attention given to what was then the main instrument of expression and communication. Furthermore, just as there was a science of physiognomy linking physical appearance to inner character, the classification of voices helped identify personality types. For example, the venerable Luisa de Carvajal in her portrait of the first Marquis of Almazán thought it necessary to clarify that this ambassador of Philip

II to the court of his cousin Rudolph of Habsburg, "had a clear and very gentle voice," by which one could deduce his excellent nature.[1]

Along with the attention to vocal timbers and sonorities, one also discovers an interest in diction and the possibility of cultivating with utmost care a particular style of pronunciation. *La flema de Pedro Hernández* (*Pedro Hernandez's Phlegmatic Humor*), published in 1657 by the royal surgeon, Marcos García, includes the following brief letter sent by a spirited Andalusian lady to too bold a suitor:

> Veruhly, suh, Ah say you ah mos' sophisticated in yaw stahl an' mannuhs, such that wuhds simply fail me. To evuhry clevuh fee-lahn that trahs t' trap me in its claws, Ah say, "Skee-at, cat!" An' that, suh, is how Ah'll ansuh you. So, g'wan an' stuff yawself with hedge hawg chops, black buhd pah, and lumps o' lahd, have yawself some rah an' oats, wash it down with cheap wahn—aw jes' th' dregs—an' then trah t' remuhdy yaw madness with a spoonful o' castuh oil. An' if, suh, you still ah wantin' some fun, g'wan an' kick up yaw heels with some uhthuh pahtnuh, since you ah jes' an insatiable swahn, an' yaw tuh-meruh-tee with me duh-suhvs no fuhthuh ansuh than this'n.[2]

Clearly, this is a burlesque (and rather forced) "reconstruction" of an accent, but what matters is to note this evidence of people's full awareness of differences in pronunciation as characteristic of certain speech communities. One can observe the same intention in such texts as a *villancico* (rustic song) imitating the speech of Guinean slaves, Luis de Góngora's *letrilla* on a sacred subject in which he apes the Spanish of Moriscos, a rough-and-tumble sailors' song set down by Eugenio Salazar echoing diverse dialects of the Mediterranean, or, for that matter, the sudden appearance of the stereotyped speech of Basques, Galicians, or peasants in plays and novellas.

An awareness of different styles of speech, not only at the phonetic level but including syntax and lexicon, made possible the identification of people's social extraction from a wide spectrum ranging from the peasantry, material for jokes, to the aristocracy, well trained in the art of speaking and its corollary, perhaps even more difficult, the art of silence. Courtly culture in sixteenth- and seventeenth-century Spain was highly oral and, as a result, can teach us much about the powers attributed to words.

No one would deny that the true courtier revealed himself by his deeds and attitudes, but above all he did so in his elegance and manner of speech. For example, a portrait of Vespasiano Gonzaga

Colonna from around 1575 presents him as an exemplary gentleman, claiming he is "a man of few words, all of which are weighty and well-considered, and whoever hears him speak will easily recognize this fact."[3] Or, in another example, the "very graceful speech" of Francisco of Portugal, the famous courtier of Philip IV's court, was one of the signs demonstrating his status as a true gentleman who "could not conceal his nature."[4]

Voice and styles of speech constituted a sort of natural distinguishing mark of the gentlemen of the court, by which they could be identified immediately, and which allowed no room for feigning. Behind such insistence on the verbal lies the ideal of the aristocrat's innate nobility, that is, the presupposition that courtliness was a natural condition of the aristocracy. Therefore, those who were not of noble blood, no matter how thoroughly they imitated aristocratic behavior, could never appear to be true gentlemen. Though the literate could learn all the rules of rhetoric, they could never attain a gentleman's eloquence because the knowledge of the former was the result of study and therefore condemned to pedantry or affectation, while the knowledge of the latter was the presumed expression of their natural preeminence. Thus, among the acts that demonstrated one's noble condition were extemporaneous poetic compositions, like mottos invented on the spur of the moment or other exhibitions of the most agile verbal wit. For this reason also some courtiers clung to their native vernacular, like the count of Gondomar who frequently used Galician, even in writing, or the duke of Cardona, who, when Charles V reportedly asked him "why he did not speak Castilian" and "always Catalan," responded "so as not to lie,"[5] ever the honest gentleman who, by his very nature, does not dissemble or deceive.

Despite this insistence on the spoken word (always so revealing) as an expression of a nobleman's inherent eloquence, courtiers nonetheless had to teach themselves how to speak and, above all, how to be silent—since moments of silence also revealed the perfect gentleman. The guides compiled for the education of young noblemen on their way to court for the first time, or who were beginning their service to a prince, insist above all on the ideal of natural, unaffected speech, proceeding thereupon to instruct in the art of conversation, undeniably the "quintessence of court life," in Francisco Rolim de Moura's words.[6]

Of course, an aristocrat always spoke the truth, being above all a man of his word, though it was not always necessary to speak in complete seriousness, since one was advised to employ his wit in good humor, without falling to the level of coarse jokes or "wounding anyone verbally or giving them occasion for regret," as Juan de Vega advised in 1548.[7] The lord of Grajal also gives advice about such complicated matters as addressing the ladies at court, indicating that, though

some may think that with women one should only offer gallantry and sweet talk (which is why some men are uncomfortable addressing them), but one should be advised that with women—all the more so with the most eminent among them—one should speak in the same fashion as with men: "How will the day turn out?"; "How did you sleep last night?"; "Were you tired when you arrived?"; or "What do you think of this country or of that house?"; and things of this kind.[8]

However, it was not always possible to speak the truth in a conversation, and silence could be more compromising than dissimulation. To resolve such a circumstance, we find in the advice to a young man headed for Alessandro Farnese's household in Flanders a subtle idea on how not to respond, "by suddenly dropping the subject and seizing upon another. Sometimes, however, this does not turn out well or is not always sufficient. Some simply claim not to know anything about the matter, but this is a great error, for they deny the truth and speak falsely."[9]

In short, the insistence by the aristocracy on the natural candor of the nobleman's speech reveals that, in the end, the spoken word was considered the most authentic form of communication because of its immediacy, compared to images and writing, where deceit was easier, since they are further removed from that which is natural. It goes without saying that, as several of the cited testimonies make clear, the use of words was, in fact, *taught* at court and noblemen's allegedly natural eloquence, improvised on the spur of the moment, was in part the fruit of such rhetorical apprenticeship. Even so, one must keep in mind the idea of immediacy attributed to speech. Images and text aspired, therefore, to nothing more than eloquence; the more sensible treatises sought to bring their teaching closer to readers by turning it into a dialogue; the best letter-writing was described as *conversable* (like a conversation), as if it allowed one to speak with those who were absent.

In the early modern period, as Foucault has shown, it was thought that there existed a relationship between signs and the realities they signified going beyond the merely expressive to the domain of the creative. Although this capacity of the sign to make the signified present, as if by sorcery, was attributed to images and texts as well, it was in spoken words where one could best observe the possibility that a representation could materialize as a real presence. The idea that saying something was not far removed from invoking whatever was being named is reflected in the power that people attributed, for example, to curses, blessings, prayers, and incantations.

In these cases it could be said that naming had an inventive aspect, being a creative act in and of itself and not merely an expression, spent as soon as it was uttered, of this idea or that desire. Thus, a certain degree of effectiveness was expected of maledictions or blessings beseeched on behalf of another person, in the same way that a prayer was a call for assistance or protection from heaven and incantations were a sort of magical summons believed capable of becoming real.

Thanks to the recent study by Testón Núñez, Sánchez Rubio, and Hernández Bermejo, *El buscador de gloria* (*The Glory Seeker*), which traces in great detail the European and American adventures of the gentleman palm reader Juan de Medina at the end of the sixteenth century, it is possible to reconstruct a divination ritual in which the spoken word in a series of incantations appears to be almighty. One incantation consisted of pronouncing the following prayer seven times: "Blessed Saint Anastasia—she made her house in the middle of the sea, which never got wet nor sank to the deep—by your holiness and virginity, show the true path in what I'll ask of thee"; later, three strange names, "Nay, May, Pay," had to be whispered in the ear of a very young virgin, followed by "said incantation, which the child, who was to call forth the person one wanted to make appear, had to repeat."[10] Of course, Juan de Medina ran into problems with the Inquisition in New Spain as a necromancer. What matters here, however, is to stress the oral mechanism fundamental to his invocations, which surely would have been less dangerous for him had he used his voice to bless or to invoke the saints rather than getting mixed up with his hocus-pocus.

Because of its expressive power and alleged truthfulness, the spoken word was expected to persuade immediately, making it especially useful for pastoral missions in Spain aimed at moving large audiences. Preachers, able to carry away the faithful by moving them to tears or provoking their ardor as effectively as the best actors, exploited all the possibilities orality offered, changing the intonation of their trained voices or switching registers according to the path they were illustrating. In *El misionero perfecto* (*The Perfect Missionary*), cited above, we find the following description of the many changes possible in the well-trained voice of Father Jerónimo López:

In addition to being clear, his voice was so flexible and well-adapted that he could easily express a variety of feelings: his voice was pleasant when he was teaching and terrible when reprehending; when exhorting, it was gentle and in conversation tender and devout. Lastly, he drove fear into sinners' hearts with the formidable thunder of his voice and with the burning lightning of his words he wounded them and pierced their conscience.[11]

Making the appropriate changes, this passage seems to be the flip side of that passage from the celebrated picaresque *Lazarillo de Tormes* in which Lázaro praises the likewise well-cared-for and experienced voice of the blind man who was his first master. The blind man knew by heart "more than a hundred prayers" and he recited them "in a deep, calm, and very sonorous tone, making the church in which he prayed resound with his voice."[12] Thus, missionaries and rogues alike were aware that a persuasive voice was one of their main tricks in the deck.

On the other hand, it is clear that the emphasis on preaching was absolutely necessary in a society dominated by illiteracy, and Christian doctrine had to be taught orally. Thus, the Mercedarian missionaries from the convent of the Virgin of the Pillar sent to the region around Jaca in the seventeenth century accompanied their preaching and visitations with curious chants which were extraordinarily simple but which served perfectly as a means of teaching the usual moral lessons. Six of these songs are known, thanks to the pamphlet *Coplas que acostumbran cantar en sus missiones los padres missionistas . . . de las montañas de Jaca* (*Songs That the Missionary Fathers . . . Sing in Their Missions in the Mountains of Jaca*) and are aimed at eradicating, respectively, the vice of hiding sins in confession, oaths, curses, gossip, lies, and indecent speech. The last song begins,

Of verbal gunshots let's be wary
by shunning speech that's lewd and foul;
to him who would an insult growl,
let's shout a clamorous "Hail Mary,"

allowing us to imagine a chorus of townsfolk led by an impassioned preacher.[13]

Nonetheless, as I have indicated, sixteenth- and seventeenth-century reliance on the spoken word should not be viewed simplistically as just a response to widespread illiteracy, for, in fact, the voice was presumed to be much more than a mere substitute for writing. As eloquent as they might have been, however, voices could not be heard by those absent and died away the moment they were pronounced, as Captain Vilhegas pointed out in his *Reading Without a Book*. For this reason one could employ images and texts, which Vilhegas's guide presents in conjunction, for, as will be recalled, both figures and letters could serve as "characters . . . for the purpose of declaring our plans, thoughts, and feelings to those who are absent."[14]

This very idea that texts and images were closely related can be found in other sixteenth- and seventeenth-century writers, though nineteenth-century prejudices viewed them as antithetical. The poet Juan de Jáuregui in his *Memorial informatorio por los pintores* (*Informative Brief for Painters*), presents the art of writing as a kind of "painting" and images as the "writing" of brush and stylus.[15] Likewise, the Cistercian monk Bernardo de Brito, in a "curious letter" possibly addressed to Juan de Silva of Toledo in the last years of the sixteenth century, places the visual and the written on the same level when speaking of the closeness between friends, perceivable with the eyes— the windows "through which the heart receives love"—or by means of letters—"through which absent friends communicate their ideas and reveal the true intimacy of their souls."[16] Brito offers seeing "present eyes" and reading "absent letters" as two parallel actions through which sentiments can be perceived, in this case, fondness between friends.

A curious illustrated report sent to Philip II from New Granada (modern Colombia) in 1584 offers a practical example of this idea.[17] That year, the indigenous leader Diego de la Torre sent the king a brief in which he related in detail the imprisonment and death of his brother the *regidor* (alderman) Pedro de la Torre, at the hands of several inhabitants of the town of Tunja who had resisted a royal inspector, a text in which de la Torre had several scenes painted illustrating what had happened. Thus, "en la forma que vuestra Majestad be" ("just as Your Majesty can see"), de la Torre himself appears in prison in chains, shackles and stocks after having refused to join the rebellion against the inspector. In an impressive scene that occupies two whole pages of the brief, one can see his dead brother surrounded by his mourning relatives, prostrated around the corpse in tearful lamentation. This expressive image does not simply illustrate the written text, but rather completes it, with the hope that it would move the king to send the requested aid.

Let us return, however, to Friar Bernardo de Brito and a passage explaining how to paint Love, where, as if we were contemplating a real painting, he describes a complex figure carefully constructed so that its diverse iconographic elements can be quite literally "read." Even today, the image remains comprehensible: he squeezes a heart in his left hand and carries a letter in his right, his eyes lowered out of modesty to suggest that fondness is maintained even from afar, and, finally, Love is completely naked.

Nakedness, here signifying the lack of egotism characteristic of true friendship, is a symbol repeated ad nauseam. Thus, the count-duke of Olivares is presented as a nude Hercules on the engraved title page of the poem *El Fernando o Sevilla restaurada* (*Fernando, or Seville Restored*), published in 1632 by Juan de Vera y Zúñiga. At one of the chief moments of favor the count-duke Gaspar de Guzmán enjoyed with Philip IV, his appearance in this fashion was intended to manifest the absence of any sort of personal interest in the service that Olivares offered the king in the government of the monarchy.

In short, images not only could represent perceptible reality, but also could express any concept, from generous love to a vassal's loyalty, regardless of how over-refined this concept might be. In other words, images in principle perhaps had a merely illustrative function, imitating nature, but presented as allegories or emblems they could also be understood at another level; that is, they were in and of themselves a source of knowledge. The nude count-duke on the engraved title page of *El Fernando* by itself transmitted the idea of the advisor's loyalty, fulfilling the same function as hundreds of written pages;

or, all the spiritual doctrine of Francis de Sales—to the exposition of which entire books were dedicated—fit neatly into the fifty-two emblems of his *Vida simbólica* (*Symbolic Life*), published in 1688 in a translation attributed to Bartolomé de Alcázar.

Up to this point, I have approached the visual as parallel to writing, following the comparison of brushes and pens so common at the time. I should add, however, now considering them separately, that images presumably offered certain benefits writing could not. In his *Eva y Ave o Maria triunfante* (*Eva & Ave, or Mary Triumphant*), António de Sousa de Macedo explains some of the advantages of images, which in his opinion arise from the fact that "painting makes a powerful impression on the mind," and he offers several examples of the use of images throughout history:

For that reason, those who tried to make Attila, the king of the Huns who sacked Europe, hateful to the population depicted him with horns; the heretics depict Catholic dignitaries in horrible ways to mislead the peasantry; the Portuguese, in the wars of King João I with Castile, represented on their banners the image of King João's own half brother, Prince João (so well loved), held prisoner as he was by the Castilians, in chains.[18]

In this passage, two things should be stressed: on the one hand, the idea that the expressiveness of images was so great they could move the spirits of those who beheld them; on the other, the possibility of their use as propaganda by kingdoms in conflict or by different faiths (noting parenthetically that Macedo's example of the latter refers to Protestants' use of images in their campaign against Roman Catholicism).

The expressive force of images was thought complete when one contemplated the living object of the gaze firsthand, although representations in effigy and other images (painted, sculpted, numismatic, and so forth) were also thought to have this power in part, in a sense not unlike the creative force of the spoken word discussed above. For example, it was recommended that pregnant women avoid viewing deformed or monstrous beings because it was assumed that such sights could influence the physical appearance of the future newborn, and that they not gaze upon grotesque paintings or sculptures for the same reason. Thus, Philip II ordered no one to speak of the "drawing of a monstrous person" sent by Vespasiano Gonzaga, "so that the Queen [Anna of Austria] should not get news of it, since it would not be good for her at this time."[19] At the opposite extreme of the visual spectrum, it was supposed that viewing the monarch in his full majesty was so dazzling that those who saw him in some ceremony became disconcerted, like the "people stunned by the presence of his royal majesty Philip II" that Alberto Pecorelli mentions in his *Il Ré Catholico* (*The Catholic King*).[20]

Physiognomic theory, which was extraordinarily widespread, was based on the principle that one's outer appearance reflected the interior virtues of the soul. Accordingly, the majesty of royalty necessarily brought with it the bewilderment of those who found themselves in its presence. Thus, monarchs had to watch their body language in every detail, as Sebastián de Ucedo explains in *El príncipe deliberante* (*The Prince in Deliberation*), when he points out that the Prince's "visage— at times composed, at times calm, at times cloudy—should imitate the heavens whose varied appearance reflects the changing weather," adding most eloquently that "it is a sign of great prudence to use the eyes in the place of the tongue."[21]

Nevertheless, as I have indicated, the expressive force of direct contemplation could be partially transferred to fashioned images, which could also move the viewer. In a famous chapter of *Errores celebrados* (*Errors of Renown*), Juan de Zabaleta expounds upon the wonderment of beholding a royal portrait, capable of making the king "present in all of his realms at the same time, causing joy" and winning the "love and respect" of his subjects.[22] Thus, with this "use of the eyes in place of the tongue," the road to propaganda through visual images is open.

Visual images serve as tools of propaganda first because of their expressiveness, the way in which they move and persuade viewers; second, because of their reproducibility, whether as paintings or sculptures, but above all, when made into engravings, of which it is possible to print numerous copies from a single plate; third, because of the ease with which they can be understood, since they require no specialized command of a written code. Of course, this last claim does not presuppose that every beholder would view the images in the same fashion or, by the same token, that the illiterate could completely decipher the complex iconographic programs that might have been encoded in festivities, triumphal entrances, decorations, and so on. What is clear, on the contrary, is that different viewers would receive the images in different ways (as different "readings"). Not every viewer could be expected to fully understand the specific icono-graphic program, although, surely, everyone could be dazzled, so to speak, by the richness, the brilliance, the color or the imaginativeness of the display.

Needless to say, in the sixteenth and seventeenth centuries writers did consider the question of the degree to which the illiterate could understand these complex images. Already then, the answer was that there were different readings according to the spectator's level of edu-cation, as one gathers from the dialogue published by Pedro Gan Giménez, between two characters—one able to read, the other illiter-ate—in which they inspect the arches built in honor of Philip III in Lisbon in 1619. Since he can neither read nor write, the character named Beltrán is incapable of understanding what we might call the hieroglyphics that fill the city: he does not carry "a student of Latin in my pocket so that when necessary, he could explain to me whatever I wanted."[23] He is not, however, a blind spectator, so to speak, before the whole display since he does identify the royal, ecclesiastical, and noble figures and even some of the allegorical ones, like Faith or Jus-tice, and is suitably dazzled by the colors and the skillful use of mate-rials with which the constructions and images were made.

Not everything pertaining to the relationship between the learned and the illiterate in the realm of iconography, however, was a matter of indoctrination or propaganda. Literate culture was familiar with images from so-called popular culture, and, what is more, the learned even used such images in a learned context for their own particular ends. Thus, in his detailed *Relación* (*Account*) sent to Philip II regard-ing the king's juridical conflict with Milan over the governorship of Lombardy, the constable of Castile, Juan Fernández de Velasco, did not hesitate to refer to "certain woodcuts in Italy customarily titled *il mondo alla roversa* [sic]" as the best way of explaining what exactly was happening in Milan.[24] In these woodcuts, "the vassal judges, and the king is judged; the horse is the driver, and the coachman pulls the carriage."[25]

The constable was evoking for the monarch an engraving that belonged to the old popular tradition known in Italy as *il mondo alla rovescia*, or "the world upside down," revealing a fluid relationship in practice between popular and learned images. Indeed, besides its familiarity with popular imagery and use of it when necessary, literate culture also consciously reflected on such images, judging them in a quite peculiar fashion. Let us examine, for example, the opinions on the matter offered by Juan de Espina, an extraordinary art collector who owned several Leonardo da Vinci codices and whose collection Charles Stuart wished to see during his visit to Madrid while still prince of Wales.

At the beginning of the 1630s, Espina proposed to Philip IV a curious musical solution for the deplorable state of the monarchy's finances, presenting himself as an intellectual or "scientific" musician, as opposed to untrained singers and instrumentalists. To explain the contrast, he imagines the effects a visit to his magnificent collection of paintings would provoke in one of "the lads who at Shrovetide paint roosters on their shuttlecocks with a little saffron and red ochre," to many of whom "it would seem the roosters could sing."[26] Of course, the young fellow from the street would not understand the subtleties of Espina's treasured paintings, many of which seem to have been from the Italian naturalist school. He would recognize, nonetheless, that his own artwork was far inferior to the Italian masters', "because we," Espina has the lad say, "paint only with our natural, untrained ability what the great men did with great study."[27] It should be noted, however, that in this passage Espina is drawing a conscious relationship between the simple carnival roosters painted with bits of cotton and gauze dipped in ink and the work of the most virtuosic brushes, thus placing both, despite their differing degrees of perfection, along the same continuum of artistic imitation of nature.

It would seem, then, that the learned recognized in these popular images a first, though imperfect, stage in the same mimesis of nature in which literate culture itself was engaged in producing its art par excellence. From this awareness of sharing with the illiterate an instrument of communication based on the desire to represent nature— regardless of the skillfulness of the representation—sprang the possibility of using images to convince and persuade, to guide viewers' behavior as part of religious proselytism or political propaganda. In other words, the existence of this common imagistic language was to be exploited as much as possible, always with the objective, of course, of producing correct readings, above all, when dealing with religious imagery after the Council of Trent.

I have already mentioned how preachers would draw parallels between the verbal imagery in their sermons and scenes represented in church paintings. This technique was, on the one hand, a way of reinforcing the words of the holy orator with visual images, but it was also a way of leading toward a correct interpretation those uneducated audience members who might misunderstand the religious imagery. It is important to point out that in the same way that offensive representations of the king were considered a crime of lese majesty, painting or treating a religious image in a mocking fashion constituted blasphemy, allowing the Inquisition to intervene against the artist or the work's owner.

Nalle has published the example of a French woodcut hanging on the wall of a shop in Requena in 1567, taken to represent the *Ecce Homo*, but which was in reality an "ill advised" young man "in shirtsleeves" who had lost everything to "gambling and whores."[28] The confusion inspired burlesque commentaries about the figure thought to be the Man of Sorrows, and, of course, the image had to be removed. According to post-Tridentine precepts on decorum in religious imagery, and given the atmosphere of paranoia in the face of the propagandistic engravings Protestants were spreading throughout half of Europe, the idea of enforcing ever greater control over images began to prevail, especially over those that could be the object of public worship in open view of the illiterate.

By means of synodical constitutions and other church ordinances for visitors, preachers, and so forth, episcopal chapters tried to regulate as much as possible both religious images and the places they were displayed, always with the aim of imposing the greatest decorum. In 1566, for example, the painter Adiosdado de Olivares wrote a series of recommendations for devotional imagery, in which he furiously attacked polychromatic and *estofado* altarpieces, among other advice of interest to us here.[29] Olivares, who seems to be writing to the prelates assembled in Salamanca for the Compostela Provincial Council, asks for the removal from inns and taverns of ornamental images "in which stories from Holy Scripture are depicted" because "in such places they are mocked rather than worshipped."[30] At the same time, he requests that all religious images ordered by municipal councils for roadside altars and hermitages should be made by artisans subject to examination, because "when poorly painted they do not inspire devotion."[31]

Olivares's recommendations, like many other texts from this period in Spain and other parts of Europe, are evidence of both the proliferation of religious imagery and concern over their erroneous interpretation by the uneducated, as Romano has explained. At the same time, they indicate the road that post-Tridentine Catholic confessionalization would follow in its attempt to direct this extra-ordinary number of images, found not only in churches but also at crossroads and even in taverns: first, through ecclesiastical visitors who would remove images considered indecorous, and second, through the imposition of a greater prior control on artists' production.

It is important to stress, however, that Catholic confessionalization did not suppress in any way the worship of images, which still is a crucial aspect of its religious practices. Rather, the Church exploited this widespread culture of images in the service of religious indoctrination. In short, what has come to be called the Catholic mission to the illiterate took full advantage of the previous representational tradition, substituting images that could seem indecorous with others in accordance with the new post-Tridentine criteria, as interpreted exclusively by the agents of the Counter reformation. Catholicism triumphed in many places, especially in rural areas, as opposed to Calvinism, to a great extent because the latter, being iconoclastic, was unable—or refused—to echo the representational tradition so ingrained in European popular culture.

It would be erroneous, however, to think that Catholic confessionalization only resorted to imagery—or to the combination of visual and oral elements. The Church was also very aware of the benefits writing could offer, not, of course, as a general instrument of dissemination in illiterate milieux, but as a tool of standardization and for establishing authorized texts. To return to the recommendations of Adiosdado de Olivares, he proposes (in addition to speaking of painted and sculpted images) enabling

any publisher of any bishopric to print any books on the manual trades or for the general well-being of the Republic, once they have been seen and examined, since they are necessary for the common good, there being many books on stone-cutting, carpentry, sculpting, painting; for silversmiths, bridle makers, or ironsmiths; books on herbs, on animals, on birds, on cosmography, the heavenly spheres, anatomy and many more. These come from France, Italy and Flanders but should be printed here to the service of God and for the good of the Republic.[32]

Perhaps because he himself was a craftsman (working in Salamanca during the middle decades of the sixteenth century), Olivares refers specifically to books printed for various sorts of artisans and other occupations, with the clear objective of propagating good models from abroad through their publication. Perhaps this was the aim of his book (never published), *Provecho de la República* (*Profit of the Republic*), for which he requested license to publish in 1555.[33] Once *vistos y examinados* ("seen and examined"), that is, subjected to strict controls to guarantee their suitability for printing, such books could be imitated after publication in Castile to the benefit of artistic decorum, since artists could improve the layout and composition of their religious works, eliminating ridiculous or poorly made figures.

What Olivares proposes relates to the possibility of controlling images by means of engravings mechanically reproduced, through the repeated inking of a single plate in order to obtain as many more or less identical copies as desired. Controlling, fixing, and disseminating are made possible thanks to the mechanical reproduction of engravings, a process similar to that of typography, the *ars artificialiter scribendi* (art of artificial writing) invented by Gutenberg in the mid-fifteenth century and which had reached its first maturity by the sixteenth and seventeenth centuries.

While Olivares indicated in 1566 the need to promote books for artisans and artists, the Jesuit Joseph Creswell, in his *Memorial para la provisión de libros católicos* (*Report on the Provision of Catholic Books*), presents Philip III in 1617 with similar arguments about books for proselytism.[34] Father Creswell was seeking royal patronage for the upkeep of the printing press at the English College of Saint Omer in Artois (then under Spanish rule), designed for the provision of books for the work the Society of Jesus was carrying out among the English crypto-Catholics.

The English Jesuit clearly assumed that the printing press had been undeniably fruitful for the Protestants, who had sown heresy in "Germany, England, and the other provinces that have been infected,"[35] and therefore, he proposes a use for typography in the Latin

Church's missions, which certainly were not proselytism exclusively by means of images or by carrying rosaries about, as the stereotype would have it. Likewise, firsthand knowledge of Protestants' editorial practices led Francisco Hurtado de Mendoza, Philip II's ambassador to the Holy Roman Emperor, to exclaim in 1573 that "we had no other recourse against the blasphemies here, than to print books to suppress them,"[36] apropos of the shipment to Flanders of a copy of the *Evangelische Inquisition* published in Dillingen by Georg Eder and printed in Italian and Dutch by Luis de Requeséns as Governor of the Low Countries.

Going beyond Hurtado de Mendoza's apparent intention simply to engage in polemic, however, Creswell gets to the bottom of the matter of typography, revealing his full awareness of why "buenos libros y cathólicos" ("good Catholic books") were the most effective means of re-Catholicizing England. Such was the case because "books could go where priests could not, to offer sound advice and make remorseful men, instructed in the teachings of the Church, search on their own for what they need."[37] Sure enough, books from Saint Omer's printing press were sent secretly to England, where they were distributed from person to person among recusants freely, in accordance with the Gospel's "Gratis accepistis et gratis date" ("Freely ye have received, freely give"; Matt. 10: 8), which was printed as a motto on the title page of each copy, "so that everybody could know that this kind of book was not to be sold."[38]

Books teach and move their readers, but they also go where Jesuit missionaries could not, thus creating a silent "Society" substituting the presence and the voice of priests. What here shines forth is typography's power of dissemination, its capacity to reach every corner with its ever-increasing number of copies, making the printed text the ideal medium for the mass dissemination of Counter-Reformation proselytism required. Since Saint Omer's presses produced books not for sale (thus his request for financial support from Philip III), Creswell did not have reason to point out another advantage of the printing press: the decrease in relative cost compared with manuscript copies.

The mechanics of typography permit a radical reduction in the number of hours required to produce a copy of a text. Therefore, the printing press implies not only an increase in the number of books but also a decrease in cost. Some writers reacted with amazement at the effect of "this new way of writing that we have witnessed and reached in our time," like Francisco Thámara in his translation of the *Livro de Polidoro Virgilio que tracta de la invención y principio de todas las cosas* (*The Book of Polydore Vergil Which Treats of the Invention and the Beginning of All Things*).[39] He affirms here that "a single man can print as much in one day as that which many could with difficulty write in a year, because of which, such an abundance of books has appeared and spread around the world that no one, no matter how poor he may be, is unable to acquire whatever work he wishes"[40]—making books more numerous, more inexpensive and, finally, more exactly like each other in appearance, since every copy comes from a single original, and if this has been set correctly, its every copy is correct, too.

It is understandable that in a period highly concerned about the correct reading of sacred texts, this power of the printing press was considered especially significant. Thus, the more obvious case of editions of the Bible aside, Teresa of Avila personally promoted the publication of the *Regla y constituciones* (*Rule and Constitutions*) of her reformed Carmelite order, affirming that "I should wish that we print these *Constitutions* because manuscript copies circulate in different forms, and some prioresses—thinking they do nothing wrong—add and remove elements as they see fit when they copy them by hand."[41]

Typography closes the text since it offers a fixed version of it, one in which, echoing Saint Teresa, nothing can be added or removed from each individual copy as seen fit, something possible with manuscripts. This condition of equality among the different copies—an ideal sullied, of course, by the possibility of the multiplication of the errata that might be found in an original prepared for printing—was crucial for the promulgation of dogmatic texts, and also of scientific and reference works, or even as a tool in the tasks of government.

Therefore, printed questionnaires were used in the production of what were known under Philip II as *Relaciones geográficas o topográficas* (*Geographical or Topographical Reports*) because it was necessary that every town council and region included in the report answer the same questions in identical order, thus facilitating the analysis of the data obtained and its subsequent elaboration as a report. In the same spirit, forty years later in 1622, the Crown disseminated on a massive scale printed copies of a *Relación de lo que el Rey . . . ha resuelto para el bien, conservación y seguridad destos Reynos* (*Report on what the King . . .*

Has Decided for the Well-Being, Preservation, and Security of These King-doms), ordering that every recipient give his opinion about proposals made by the new king, Philip IV. Use of printed forms, even among the documents used in legal proceedings, helped standardize information, which saved time and eased its processing. For example, documents from inquisitorial trials—such as the 1572 proceedings against Martín Martínez, a professor of Hebrew—bring to light the different forms used, such as the form for confirmation of witnesses or the one recording seizures of property.[42] Thus, one can find forms that today seem so habitual, with blank spaces to be filled out in each case, such as the following:

In the town of Valladolid, the _____th day of the month of _____ of one thousand, five hundred and _____, in the presence of the Lord Inquisitors _____; _____, resident of _____, having been called to appear in the court at _____ . . .[43]

Though typography did not always enjoy the good reputation that nineteenth-century historiography would have imagined (as I have suggested in the previous chapter), one cannot deny that the possibility of having access to a greater number of books with more reliable, standardized texts at relatively lower prices made the printed book unstoppable in its steady advance in the early modern period. Those who might have felt the need to propagandize with multiple, inexpensive copies resorted to the printing press (churches or crowns facing off in polemics over basic principles in pamphlets, manifestos, and accusatory writings) as did those who required carefully prepared standardized texts for the work germane to their discipline (mathematicians or astronomers with their tables, experts in classical literature, and biblical exegetes or dogmatizing theologians with their corrected copies full of marks rectifying typographical and interpretive errors). Those who sought fame or admission to the select Parnassuses of the "Republic of Letters" likewise took their works to the printing press as the surest way of obtaining the wide dissemination that celebrity demanded. Those who wished to take full advantage of the new business of editions intended to satisfy the tastes of increasingly wider audiences, turned to the printing press and abandoned the workshops dedicated to the production of manuscript copies which had flourished in the fourteenth and fifteenth centuries.

Nevertheless, the expansion of typography did not imply the disappearance of the manuscript copy, which survived in the early modern period and, hardly extinct, even developed new uses. While the *ars artificialiter scribendi* served to disseminate and standardize, the so-called writing *ad vivum*—in other words, manuscripts—had specialized applications that responded, for example, to the greater solemnity or privacy of a given text or to the need to maintain an open discursive structure.

In this sense, the privacy of the manuscript represents the flip side of the dissemination of printed texts, which, being widely divulged, came to seem common and lost some of their distinctiveness, a uniqueness recoverable through the medium of handwritten texts—or at least ones that seemed to be handwritten. For example, the presentation copies of a printed work would be on parchment rather than on the paper of the regular copies, and might even be illuminated or colored to give them the solemn air of a manuscript. Or, the members of a poetic academy might circulate their compositions in only a handful of manuscript copies in order to make them all the rarer, distancing them from the common printed text, according to the very wishes of their finicky authors and readers.

This degree of solemnity and privacy is greatest in the case of holograph manuscripts, written in the author's own hand and entrusted only to the eyes of friends and family. In correspondence between members of the court, it is possible to gauge the esteem one correspondent feels for another by the number of lines written in his own hand. In short, while printed matter implies in principle a wider readership, the manuscript dominates the realm of private and deferential writing, as can be seen in that genre of instructions, reminders and advice that aristocrats composed for their heirs, and to which I have already referred when discussing the oral tradition in the life of the court. With the exception of Juan de Silva's instructions printed in 1612 (of which only one printed copy apparently survives, alongside the numerous manuscript copies that have been preserved), all those collections of advice and admonitions appear in texts that circulated in manuscript form. This was the case because they were intended exclusively for the noble members of the court, as opposed to the general rules of civility that could be found in the great treatises on courtly behavior, which were in fact printed, making their precepts universally known, both by true gentlemen and by those who wished to imitate them in their manners and gestures.

In addition, however, these manuscript compendia of instructions would be repeatedly modified in order to adjust the information to changes at court, explaining, for example, how to adapt to new figures such as that of the king's favorite, who in the seventeenth century had gained significantly increased political prominence. Thus, a form of continuous "rewriting" necessarily develops, which leads to (for example) the advice penned in 1548 by Juan de Vega, lord of Grajal, being "adicionada" (supplemented) by Juan de Silva, count of Portalegre, in 1592, glossed subsequently by Diego Sarmiento de Acuña, count of Gondomar, by Francisco Rolim de Moura and by an anonymous author who glosses them all in 1644 and who, finally, advises the young courtier to read Luis de Góngora's poetry. Manuscript copies prove ideal in this situation, since they readily accommodate rewritings, by not fixing the text in a definitive, printed form and thus allowing for its continual reelaboration.

As we will see in a following chapter, these manuscript copies circulated in specific circles of copyists and readers, which, though they could not provide the massive dissemination offered by the printing press (not desired in these cases anyway), nonetheless guaranteed swift, remarkably thorough distribution within those circles. For now, however, let us keep in mind the idea that writing—whether *ad vivum* or printed—possessed qualities that made it especially suitable for, as Captain Vilhegas would have said, "declaring oneself" to those who are absent both in space and time. Thus, people in the early modern period were fully aware that the fixing of ideas, deeds, or emotions on different media—but above all on paper, common since the middle of the Middle Ages—would allow them to overcome distance and time in the very best condition.

Although an autograph letter composed by a courtier might be considered superior and a poorly written polemical pamphlet vulgar, both were tools for conquering geographic distance. In addition, however, they could also be collected, compared, brandished in a debate, archived, restored, cited, or subjected to whatever operation one could imagine possible with a form of record-keeping that by its very nature best lent itself to preservation. We are reminded that writing could surpass images, regardless of how marvelous these might be, by the *letrilla* mentioned at the beginning of Chapter 1 about the portrait of the prince of Savoy that in the end was unidentifiable because no one had thought to inscribe the name of the personage, but whose fame nonetheless could be restored with "a sword made from a goose's plume / and bolstered by a paper shield." An example of how writing was likewise able to overcome the echo of the most persuasive oral discourse is to be found in the above-mentioned *Diálogos* (*Dialogues*) by Pedro de Navarra Labrit, when he pronounces that "the spoken word serves only him who is present and can hear," while writing "lasts and always speaks" and serves "him who is absent, present and yet to come and likewise him who is deaf and mute."[44]

The praises of writing sung in the sixteenth and seventeenth centuries were many. Some of them were invoked in the opening pages of this chapter. It is worthwhile to now recall two others: the first appears at the beginning of the *Museo o biblioteca selecta del . . . Marqués de Montealegre* (*Museum or Choicest Library of the . . . Marquis of Montealegre*) by José Maldonado y Pardo, in which he assures the reader that "if there were not books made available and preserved for present and future ages, human labor, reduced to the precepts of a naked tradition, would be fruitless."[45] The second is the Castilian proverb collected by Gonzalo de Correas in his *Vocabulario de refranes* (*"Dictionary of Proverbs"*): "Hablen cartas, callen barbas" ("Let letters speak; from whiskers not a squeak").

Although speech and images could also communicate and preserve knowledge, writing surely seized the most favored place with regard to the preservation of information in the early modern period. Without books, literate knowledge would have been inexplicable—a form of knowledge established from antiquity as a tradition that (paraphrasing Maldonado and Pardo) ornamented itself with books in a continuous process of glossing, commenting, and citing authorities and classic texts. Without writing, modern forms of government would have been impossible, relying as they do on deeds, bulls, manifestos, stamped paper, and the steady development of official dealings increasingly dependent on the consultation of written documents to the detriment of the practice of holding hearings. To paraphrase Manuel de Faria e Sousa's portrait of Philip II, the paperwork monarch par excellence ("almost always leaning upon his desk, pen in hand, writing over the span of his lifetime what would require much time to read"[46]), the modern government office would be inconceivable and inexplicable without pens and desks.

The significant stamp that writing left on Spanish culture in the sixteenth and seventeenth centuries represents the central subject matter of the two following chapters of this book. In them, however, images and speech will not completely disappear, for they remained present also in that specific realization of writing which is reading. Writing continued to maintain a lively and intense relationship with those other two forms of communication, knowledge, and memory, perhaps because in writing, too, there resided something of that essential creativity which we have seen manifested in a voice that upbraids or blesses and in the powerful images whose contemplation was propitiatory.

Thus, Juan Bautista Cardona, like other censors, found it necessary to strike out the names of heresiarchs, as if the relapsed soul might rise again from behind the written letters. Thus, Jorge de Ataíde, head chaplain of Philip II in Portugal, gave to the countess of Atalaia some silver bracelets which alleviated certain stomach ailments, "ventusidades manencónicas" (melancholic windiness), and which, like an incantation, had inscribed on the inside the mysterious letters "† DIA † B † S. ABN † † S † H † CEBE † R † S" and on the outside "† ZDI A † BI † Z † SA B † ZQ F † BE † RS †."[47] Thus, the architect Francisco de Mora declared in Teresa of Avila's canonization proceedings that she had cured one of his servants with a small fragment of the saint's writing he had preserved as a relic because her miraculous powers had transferred naturally to the paper and ink. Thus, finally, the illiterate preacher Juan de Collega, the subject of Nalle's study, always carried with him a printed booklet containing a few prayers, which he believed would serve as protection on deserted mountain passes, as if it were a talisman.

Chapter 3

Natural History of the Written Text: Authors, Copyists, Printers, Booksellers, and Readers

Perhaps the best evidence of the mark writing—or, better said, reading and writing—left on the culture of Golden Age Spain lies in its definitive conversion into a wholly quotidian reality even for the illiterate. As is well known, a classic method for evaluating the extent of illiteracy in the sixteenth and seventeenth centuries is the systematic analysis of large numbers of public documents in which one of the executors declared that he did not know how to write, making it necessary to rely on a witness to sign in his name. Though it is not a very accurate method for knowing the full reality of illiteracy, it is important here to stress that it surely demonstrates the high degree of familiarity with writing among the illiterate, who would go to the clerk's office as if it were the most usual thing, declaring themselves unable to write.

In early modern Spain, writing became inseparable from public institutions of religion and justice, although, of course, there was still very ample space for customs, usages, and styles based on oral tradition. Power in the early modern period was founded on writing, on desks and pens, regardless of the level of literacy of vassals, who had to obey their lords within the period's wide spectrum of legal obligations. For this reason, many of the revolts and popular uprisings so frequent at the time had as one of their first objectives the destruction of written documents and measuring instruments, as if it were a ritualistic act full of symbolism. It is also true, though, that illiterate peasants availed themselves of the justice system's written procedures in order to engage in interminable lawsuits against their lords (some of which could last for over a hundred years), taking full advantage of the delays caused by the continuous flow of documents and indictments.

In addition, however, writing began to conquer many other spaces, from the open spaces of streets and squares to the most enclosed spaces of people's characters and inner thoughts. The verses cited in Chapter 1 in which *Fuente Ovejuna*'s Leonelo spoke of the abundance of signs that had taken over Salamanca, where "although one might be highly skilled at reading, / he'll find that placard Babel quite misleading," are a good indication of the expansion of writing in the urban landscape. It goes without saying that Salamanca was not the only city conquered by writing in this fashion, as Antonio Castillo Gómez has shown in his study on Renaissance Alcalá de Henares.

The abundant inscriptions carved or painted on façades, walls, bridges, fountains, and doors are combined with the edicts, placards, lists of indulgences, and paper notices pasted on the walls of the most frequented places, not to mention the primitive ads for business of all kinds. Going along a street in Barcelona in Part Two of Cervantes's book, Don Quixote finds the sign "Aquí se imprimen libros" ("Books Printed Here") announcing a print shop, which he enters only to find the counterfeit *Quixote,* a sequel penned spuriously by a certain Avellaneda in imitation of Cervantes's creation. Juan de Espinosa's elementary school in Madrid announced itself similarly in 1590 with two large signs that read: "Aquí se enseña a leer y escribir" ("Reading and Writing Taught Here"). Finally, in the *Tercera parte de Guzmán de Alfarache* (*Third Part of Guzmán of Alfarache*) by Félix Machado, marquis of Montebelo, there is an exceedingly curious sign "in large, beautiful letters" that invites "all those curious persons who should wish to be fortune-tellers to find in this house one who would teach them to tell the future in less than a quarter hour, at the price of a silver piece, without any magic or other means condemned by our holy Catholic faith."[1]

Among this veritable profusion of writings—capable of confusing even the Licenciate Leonelo—we also find inscriptions commemorating the visit of important personages to this or that place, such as entrances to inns, which according to Francisco de Fresneda were decorated from the beginning of the seventeenth century with inscriptions that would read, "The Prince, Duke, or Archbishop of Such-and-Such passed by this place."[2] A similar case is that of graffiti, such as those which seem to have been a favorite object of condemnation for the *misionero perfecto* Jerónimo López, who preached in Valencia and Salamanca against the "obscene and lascivious words and images" that appeared on the walls of streets and squares in both cities.[3] The effect of his sermons was immediate: in Valencia, several gentlemen and López himself left the church directly to erase the walls—armed with a bucket of whitewash and brushes—"especially along the road to the sea leading to the town of El Grau, where very indecent things were written and painted; there, over what they crossed out, they wrote morally profitable texts wherever space allowed."[4] Thus, the space now erased was again occupied by writing, though of an edifying sort.

As I have indicated, however, writing entered daily life not only through its strengthened presence in streets and squares. Increasing familiarity with writing also led to the conquest of people's inner space, making it possible to characterize individuals based on their particular reading tastes. This claim does not imply simply that a certain number of readings could be ascribed—as historians typically have—to the members of particular social and professional groups, thereby limiting discussion to lawyers', doctors', or architects' books; on the contrary, it was understood then that one could define a reader's character by the genres or the titles he preferred to read.

A good example of this method of determining individuals' characters based on reading tastes can be found in the questionnaire created in 1589 to choose the perfect candidate for marriage to the heiress of Juan Álvarez de Toledo, fourth Count of Oropesa. It is a brief list of questions about the potential groom, regarding, for example, the source and amount of his income, any litigation his house might be involved in, or his place in the line of succession, along with his virtues, defects, pastimes, and tastes. Among the latter questions appears one inquiring after "the kinds of books and writing preferred" by the aspirant to heirdom in the House of Oropesa.[5]

Some of the answers to this curious questionnaire have been preserved, by means of which we know of a certain candidate's preference for books in Italian and chivalric romances and another's fancy for works on cosmography. What is of greatest interest here, however, is the instrumental role given to a question about personal reading habits, which furthermore appears in a hardly cursory document, free of floridity, being absolutely crucial in decisions about the future of an aristocratic family. This questionnaire from 1589 not only reveals that gentlemen were in the habit of reading but, more important, that people expected to be able to know others' characters through familiarity with their reading preferences.

Having confirmed the significant increase in the presence of writing in sixteenth- and seventeenth-century Spain, we should now investigate these texts' circulation, from their initial production by different authors, passing through intermediaries such as copyists, printers, and booksellers, to their eventual consumption by the reading public. Indeed, this scheme is circular and, despite its complexity, reproducible, since reading engendered writing and vice versa.

If we heed the little treatise, "De la forma en que se deue tener en leer los authores" ("On the Way in Which One Should Read Authors"), included in the *Rethórica en lengua castellana* (*Rhetoric in the Castilian Language*) by Miguel de Salinas, we discover that reading for the learned was an activity that would ideally translate at once into writing. The approach to reading proposed by Salinas consisted of taking selective notes from the different books one was reading in order to compile long lists of commonplaces "to be free to use them whenever necessary."[6] Thus, this system reduced the process of reading to the objective of eventual citation, an approach directly related to the reading of *auctoritates*, though going beyond its scholastic origins. It became a practical reality in numerous notebooks, books of memoranda, or handwritten collections of excerpts. Some of these have been preserved, such as the sixteenth-century *Alveolus* (*Honeycomb*) by Antonio Agustín and the *notata* (notes) by Alvar Gómez de Castro, Pedro Velázquez, and Juan Vázquez de Mármol, which reflect their successive readings of authoritative texts or others, over the course of many years or even a lifetime, beginning with the lessons they heard as students.[7] In this regard, an observation of Juan Méndez Nieto's in his *Discursos medicinales* (*Medicinal Discourses*) is pertinent, namely, that there were Arts and Theology students in Salamanca who never read a single printed book: "having enough with notebooks, they are passed, seeming at times better bachelored than the rest."[8]

Another way of reading among the learned, very similar to this style of annotations, was the composition of brief summaries of the books one was reading. A third approach was to jot down handwritten glosses in the margins of the main text, known at the time as *marginar* or *margenar* one's readings. All these annotations could subsequently become the basis for a new text, something unsurprising if we remember that intellectual creation was largely understood as a long gloss or commentary on previously established authorities, even in the case of poetry, where it was essential to evoke traditional commonplaces in preference to the formulation of new turns of thought.

Upon the foundation of this pile of notes, summaries and hand-written glosses, an author would begin by composing his drafts. (According, incidentally, to Agustín de Rojas Villandrando in his *El buen repúblico* [*The Good Republic*], August was the best month to "undertake the writing of new works."[9]) If one is to believe Manuel de Faria e Sousa in his *El gran justicia de Aragón* (*The Great Chief Magistrate of Aragon*, Madrid, 1650), authors usually composed two drafts, although he himself laments that "I was never so fortunate that I could avoid at least three drafts, and in some cases four, five or even more."[10] From these drafts would emerge the final version (our "original"), which the Portuguese chronicler calls *en limpio* (the fair copy) to be read in public, copied in manuscripts, or taken to a printing shop for publication.

The rhetoric of modesty expected of writers who considered themselves cultured demanded that they insistently deny any aspirations for public recognition, since satisfaction with their own virtue allegedly precluded any need for fame, which depended on the opinions of others. Nonetheless, early modern authors did wish to win this general fame just as much as the possible profits from the sale of their books or protection from the powerful obtained through their writing. About this matter Cervantes had something to say in the prologue to the second part of *Don Quixote*, where he affirms that "one of the greatest [temptations] is for [the devil] to put it in a man's head that he can write and print a book with which to win as much fame as money earned and as much money as fame."[11]

Though the temptation may have been great, there were many difficulties, however, before seeing one's book printed. I speak of typography because, as we already know, this was the surest way of winning fame and money given the possibility of turning the book into an object of mass consumption, with print-runs averaging around a thousand copies. In his *Cómo se hacía un libro en nuestro Siglo de Oro* (*How a Book Was Made in Our Golden Age*), González de Amezúa summarizes the main steps in the production of a printed book in the

Kingdom of Castile. First of all, it was necessary to obtain the approval of the Council of Castile and of the episcopal vicariate; second, a *licencia y privilegio*[12] was to be issued guaranteeing the author (or whoever owned author's rights) that no one could publish the work without their permission.

Once these initial formalities were successfully completed, the work could now be printed, in principle at the author's expense, a contract having been drawn up detailing all manner of circumstances related to the printing process, including delivery deadlines, the size of a print-run, paper quality, fonts, and even the number of proofs that should be corrected, where and by whom. If the author could not pay for the publication of his manuscript, a common occurrence, he would have to find a third person who could, usually in exchange for a dedication of the work; or, he could sell his rights to the printer, a bookseller, or any private individual who could finance the enterprise. Once the book was printed, it would be reexamined by the Council of Castile, first to correct mistakes and to make certain no changes had been introduced in the text since its initial approval other than the addition of so-called paratexts (royal and ecclesiastical imprimaturs, privilege leaf, dedication, fe de erratas, and so forth), and, second, to determine what the *tasa* (official fee) should be, that is, the highest price at which the book could be sold. It is important, however, to mention that for the publication of minor texts, of one or only a few pages—referred to with such terms as *papeles, menudencia* or *receteria*[13]—that did not require a *licencia y privilegio*, it was not necessary to embark upon such a long process; to judge by the numerous legal claims and financial declarations, their publication required only a commercial contract between the individual and the printer.

Thus, the original manuscript became a printed text, now able to circulate commercially, as long as people chose to read it. Readers' ability to choose worried both the Crown and the Church, which undoubtedly expected much from the printing press's ability to disseminate and discipline. At the same time, however, both feared that the extraordinary potential of print could be turned against their idea of political and doctrinal orthodoxy. As a consequence, a system of pre-publication censorship was instituted, as were indices of forbidden books and inquisitorial visits aimed at controlling the consumption of books, which was always suspect.

Books would be typically sold unbound, or at most with coarse paper covers, and it was their new owner who was responsible for binding them. The sale of books was the domain of booksellers, who operated from shops or from street stands, but it was also that of printers, many of whom were also booksellers. Even authors could sell their own books, and then there was also the network, yet little studied, of peddlers and street vendors who frequented fairs and wandered along streets with their load of novelties. Finally, a fairly common way of acquiring books was by purchasing them at the auctions of the possessions of the deceased, which seems to have been an extraordinarily important second-hand marketplace, as it were.

Books came into homes by any of these paths, to end up in such varied places as in nets that hung from rafters so mice could not gnaw on them, on shelves in a *librería* (the name used generally for the modern Spanish *biblioteca*, or library), or in chests and drawers. It was not necessary, however, to own books, since they could be rented or borrowed, as was common practice. Nor was it necessary to know how to read, as we shall see, to know the contents of a book. At the beginning of his *Rimas varias* (*Diverse Rimes*) an amused Vicente Gusmão Soares, placed this letter to the reader:

Nosey friend, if you've borrowed me, read and keep quiet, and since you'll not thus be praising my fine points, then likewise, as if a courteous guest in another's home, keep to yourself my defects. But if you've bought me, I am yours, so do as you please; I only forewarn you that it is folly to speak ill of something, just because you paid money for it. And I ask that you convey to my noble lords, who judge what they do not understand and pronounce their opinion according to the rules of their own taste and by the laws of their own partialities, my grateful salutations. Farewell.[14]

Among all the entities that participated in the complex process of publishing, two have become the preferred object of study among recent historians: on the one hand, printers and on the other, the addressees of the book's dedication. Regarding the latter, it is of interest above all to clarify their relationship with authors, a new form of give-and-take that situates them in something more than just a simple relationship of patronage and reveals how the aristocracy and the politically powerful, eager to benefit from the increased consumption of printed books, sought after the propagandistic powers of the printing press. Regarding the printers, thanks to analysis of manuscripts used in print shops, it has been demonstrated that their role was essential, since they were responsible for numerous modifications while the original manuscript was in their hands, whether or not they had purchased publishing rights from the author, changes that would be fundamental to the final shape of the text available to readers.

Among the printer's contributions, most notable are everything related to the mise-en-page, the use of punctuation, the writing of indices and tables of contents, the alteration of general titles or chapter epigraphs: all changes that would assist readers' subsequent assimilation of the material. In a letter to the count of Roca on the occasion of the publication of Roca's *El embaxador* (*The Ambassador*) from the Seville printing house of Francisco de Lira, the duke of Sessa praises the edition, remarking that "I have always thought that what happens with houses happens also with books, namely, that a house graced with a pleasing exterior, light and gardens makes one wish to live there, just as an artfully prepared edition makes one wish to read it."[15]

It is also true that the errata that impeded or spoiled a proper reading of a text were attributable to the printing process. Contemporaries consistently complained of printers' failure sufficiently to proofread, and of their practice of putting into circulation texts with mistakes due to the author's carelessness in going over the proofs or the ignorance or negligence of the printer's own proofreaders. In 1572, Juan Vázquez de Mármol, who had served for years as proofreader for the Council of Castile, called attention to the errata that had slipped into the Castilian edition of *Imagen de la vida christiana ordenada por diálogos* (*Image of Christian Life Arranged in Dialogues*) by Friar Heitor Pinto, remarking that "although it is true that a reader of good judgment could understand some passages with errors"—the argument printers used in their defense—"books are read equally by people of good judgment as by those of poor judgment."[16] Concerned about the matter, he expressly cites several such errata attributable to typesetters and wonders what those of poor judgment might make of a passage like, "yo soy hombre tan bien como Dios es Dios" ("I am as good a man as God is a god") instead of "yo soy hombre también, como Dios es Dios" ("I too am a man, just as God is God").

Thus, for better or for worse, a printer's particular style could become unmistakable, and, even if there was an attempt at concealment, experienced readers could discern telltale evidence. For example, in his correspondence with the duke of Sessa in early 1630, Lope de Vega announces the publication of Francisco de Quevedo's satirical *Chitón de las Taravillas* (*The Chatterbox Husher*), which appeared anonymously and with a false imprint:

> *The Chatterbox Husher* is most accurate in its assessment of the world. . . . Francisco de Aguilar read it to me in a coach by the river one afternoon. There are five printed signatures, with somewhat large letters, and judging by the ornamental initials, which are the largest, it is clear that the book was published in Madrid, though it says "at Huesca, Aragon." Father Nisseno Basilio, who had also seen the book, forewarned me and told me the printer was Bernardino de Guzmán.[17]

Moreover, the evident economic interest of printers, booksellers, and others who financed the publication of books—who thought of books as essentially commercial objects—seems to have been responsible for an enormously important alteration in the traditional relationship between genres and social groups. That change is what Quevedo refers to in his *Sueños* (*Dreams*) when he places a bookseller in Hell because, in the condemned man's words, "we unloaded at bargain prices books in the vernacular translated from Latin, so that now fools manage to learn cheaply what only the wise held dear in the past; now for Latinizing even lackeys are able, and, if you want a Castilian Horace, go look in a stable."[18]

Commercial interest led to the vulgarization of the classics, turning them into matter that could be sampled, so to speak, by even the lackeys. From the contrary point of view, however, the printing press also served to make the creations of the illiterate familiar to gentlemen and ladies, who immersed themselves in the idle entertainments of popular culture more suitable for the lackeys and stable boys whom Quevedo mocks as Latinists. In short, print shops did not disregard the ample popular demand for printed material and therefore used their presses for the publication of popular texts—*pliegos* (chapbooks), *coplas* (popular songs), *romances* (ballads), and so forth—that groups higher in the social hierarchy could thus consume. With his elitist view of social class, Quevedo perceived the availability of such texts as a sort of subversion deserving infernal condemnation.

On the other hand, it is important to highlight the fact that, weighing down upon Quevedo's judgment and upon the marked polemic over good or bad reading material (chivalric romances or plays versus morally instructive works, for instance) was the awareness that the printing press had created a new reading public. The novelty lay not only in the emergence of a large number of potential readers (a circumstance related to the printing press's powers of dissemination) but also in the fact that the readership of one text or another might have virtually nothing in common, encompassing people of different social extraction, gender, and age, in contrast with previous periods when there was greater differentiation among authors' or texts' presumable audiences.

Everyone who publishes books knows that they can fall into anyone's hands, even those of people whom they would not wish to have reading their books, both the learned and the unschooled, both the "judi-" and the "gulli-," as the fairy Urganda the Unknown puts it in her dedicatory "broken-end" couplets addressed "To the Book of Don Quixote de la Mancha" at the beginning of Cervantes's first edition.[19] Thus, it should come as no surprise that Vicente Gusmão Soares would direct an invective against part of his audience in the letter "A quien lee" ("To the reader") prefacing his *Rimas* (*Rhymes*) quoted above nor that Marcos García could address his future reader with bewilderment in *La flema de Pedro Hernández* (*The Phlegmatic Humour of Pedro Hernández*), thus: "you are so diverse that I might as well call you a chameleon, an inconstant little creature always changing the color of its dress."[20]

Current trends in the history of the book have reduced the autonomy of what used to be considered the all-powerful figure of the author, on the one hand, by acknowledging the active role of dedicatees and, above all, printers, or on the other, by conferring increased importance on the role of reader. Starting from the Enlightenment presupposition of the triumphant, individual authorial genius who wrote with a systematic program in mind, nineteenth-century critics imagined that the sixteenth- and seventeenth-century author was a sort of heroic creator who put forth his ideas to an audience that received them submissively, thus reducing readers' role to mere passive subjects indoctrinated or enthralled by writers of greater or lesser brilliance.

One of the most curious printed works of sixteenth-century Spain is the rare book published in Seville that reports the literary contest held among several authors from that city celebrated in honor of Saint John the Evangelist in the presence of Archbishop Alonso Manrique in December of 1531.[21] As is well known, this type of competition enjoyed great favor in the Golden Age, when the sharpest wits among men of letters imitated the chivalric model of feigned combat, some of whom, undoubtedly, were already well trained in the rich university tradition of *palestras* (the "lists," i.e., academic literary competitions).

The printed work of the 1531 tournament, however, is remarkable in that it established a very special relationship between the text and its unknown future readers, closely following the customary terminology of chivalric exercises. When the competition poems were printed, it was decided to conceal the name of the winner so as not to dishonor, as the text explains, those other poet-jousters who had not been rewarded with the "jewel," or prize. Furthermore, the arrangement of authors and poems in the printed version could not be used to deduce the winner's identity since the order was determined by lots, "printing first the poem among six whose lot was first drawn and second the one whose lot was drawn second and so on."[22] The reader was to "decide the victor":

the reader who would wish to be a good judge should first read every poet's work and then assign to each the place that according to his opinion he thinks each deserves. In this way, he who receives no prize will have no complaint against the judges nor will the Lord Judges be judged by those who assume the role of judge; so let him who wishes to make the effort of reading decide the victor as he sees fit and write out everyone's poems in whatever order he wishes, for it is in his hands.[23]

This tournament, then, far from coming to a conclusion at the moment of its celebration, was repeated again and again each time new readers could get their hands on a copy of the poems, which had now begun to circulate in printed form. Upon the readership was conferred the title of judge over the single combat waged between authors in pursuit of the recognition due their wit, though the prize was not the habitual jewel or silk badge but rather being designated victor by the reader and coming to occupy "the place that according to his opinion he thinks each deserves."

In short, in the same way that it is impossible to understand early modern literary creation without recalling that system of continuous compilation of glosses, summaries, and annotations on authorities and commonplaces, as I have already indicated, it does seem that the early modern reader was limited to seeking understanding of a given author's thesis or to discovering the key to the author's narrative, as would have been expected in the nineteenth century. On the contrary, reading a book in the sixteenth and seventeenth centuries could imply a much more dynamic role for readers, who in one way or another participated actively in the process of reading, becoming not simply judges but almost co-authors of what they read.

One can find texts that encouraged open readings; that is, they allowed readers to choose the sections of the text they wished to read, disregarding whole chapters or paragraphs. Thus, in *Amor con vista* (*Prudent Love*), a curious narrative published in 1634 by Juan Enríquez de Zúñiga, one finds a note on folio 40 with this warning: "The dream begins. Whoever wishes to continue with the story, turn to the third section," which leads us to folio 73.[24] Likewise, in the *Testimonio auténtico y verdadero de las cosas notables que pasaron en la . . . muerte de . . . Phelipe II* (*True and Authentic Testimony of the Noteworthy Things That Occurred upon the . . . Death of . . . Philip II*), Cervera de la Torre marks with asterisks the exact words of those who attended to the king at the moment of his death, while his own glosses are marked with a cross, so as to allow a reader interested only in the original testimonies to find them by skipping from asterisk to asterisk.

One way of "performing" a reading, that is, of transforming the text by "re-creating" it at the very moment of reading—is connected with the basic knowledge of commonplaces and literary authorities that authors and readers immersed in the same literate culture shared. Thus, readers would complete the meaning of the text offered by the author by searching in their own memory, so to speak, for the allusions and commonplaces the author used, which readers would "recognize," rather than learning it as if for the first time. This way of completing a text can only be understood if we recall the culture of literary *auctoritates* discussed earlier and recognize that for many genres, an author was not valued because of the text's innovativeness but, on the contrary, because of its skillful redeployment of already wellknown and well-established ideas and thematic material.

A second form of what I call "performing" a reading is related to practices associated with the then widely read literature of a religious nature, especially the technique of so-called mental prayer. This consisted of the ritualized reading of one chapter or passage from a pious text, followed by meditation on a religious image that should be present so as to complete visually the sense of the words: For this reason, this kind of reading was typically carried out in private oratories before a private altar or, for that matter, simply before a printed engraving in some other private space. The result was a kind of contemplation in which the effects of the written and visual joined together.

Finally, we should consider how extraordinarily widespread reading out loud was in the sixteenth and seventeenth centuries, as Chartier has pointed out, something that today has been completely replaced by our practice of silent reading, although, of course, this latter form of reading also existed in the early modern period. By lending their voices to the text, readers enjoyed a more central role, than that of submissive receptors that nineteenth-century historians of literature presupposed. Evidence for the practice of reading out loud is numerous, the first being perhaps punctuation marks, which in early modern texts seem to set guidelines for oral readings, since they respond to elocutionary, rather than syntactic criteria.[25]

Among literary testimonies of oral reading, one finds the famous passage in *Don Quixote* where the harvesters listen to the reading of books of chivalry in the inn or the equally famous advice about "the techniques one should observe when reading this book [out loud]" offered in *Celestina*.[26] Likewise, at the beginning of his *Libro de la vida y milagros de S. Inés* (*Book of the Life and Miracles of Saint Agnes*), Friar Álvaro de Hinojosa y Carvajal places the following warning:

It is said, pious reader, that the lioness gives birth to a coarse, formless offspring, whose limbs cannot be distinguished, and then, by licking it, little by little she shapes it with her tongue, giving it new form. This, my book, is a part of my mind that today emerges into the world, to everyone's eyes coarse and formless, but the benevolent reader will with his tongue carry out the duties of the merciful mother, giving the text new form.[27]

Further evidence of this very important phenomenon of oral readings would be (among many other possibilities) Teresa of Avila's calling to memory in her autobiography the books of chivalry that she listened to as a child in the company of her mother; or the passage cited by Prieto Bernabé in Gonzalo Fernández de Oviedo's *Libro de la cámara real* (*Book of the Royal Chamber*) about the books that were to be kept in Prince Juan's chamber "to be read when he is eating or at night in winter after dinner or at other times, by whomever his highness commands to read";[28] or the charming comment that appears in the *Doctrina del Príncipe de Piamonte* (*Teaching of the Prince of Piedmont*) about the courtiers of Louis of Savoy in the Empress Isabel's court at Madrid, who "in wintertime would read chronicles and noble histories to him" after dinner;[29] or, finally, Luisa de Carvajal's recalling listening to her uncle, the marquis of Almazán, read out loud to her "the Holy Scripture and Holy Doctors of the Church," surrounded by the other members of her family and the servants of the house.[30]

Besides taking into consideration the expressiveness attributed to the spoken word in the period, the practice of reading out loud can be explained as a sort of *industria* (ingenuity), to use a favorite expression of the "perfect missionary" Jerónimo López, who recommended reading passages from Scripture out loud to the parishioners as a complement to preaching. On the one hand, it is clear that oral readings enabled the illiterate to become familiar with texts, whether religious or secular, that otherwise they could not assimilate, pointing to a means by which literate culture spread among the illiterate. On the other hand, however, oral delivery of texts could also be understood as a means of controlling reading, a matter particularly significant in the case of devotional readings. Here, the reader, whether a priest or some person of authority such as the marquis of Almazán, becomes an intermediary between the religious texts and the common folk by guarding the correctness of the interpretations that those texts might be given. Viewed in this light, reading out loud would appear to be a fully self-conscious strategy intended to counter free readings of texts—an activity considered highly dangerous in this period of counter-reform—and not the expression of a cultural inertia that preserved pre-modern practices.

The very same observations can be made regarding the circulation of manuscript copies after the invention of the printing press, a cultural activity that did not represent a residue, so to speak, of medieval customs, but on the contrary a specific response to concrete contemporary needs. In the period, it is common to find the expression *corre manuscrito* (it circulates in manuscript form) to refer to this continuous movement of handwritten copies.

I have already explained how the handbooks of advice that the great courtiers composed for their heirs were disseminated via manuscript rather than in print because it was necessary that their specific content be kept somewhat private and also because they were texts continuously rewritten in order to account for the changing circumstances at court. The manuscript copy proved especially appropriate, both for its comparative solemnity and privacy and for its structural flexibility, permitting the easy incorporation of modifications.

To serve this and other demands for handwritten copies (such as satires, libels, poetry, plays, announcements, genealogies, chronicles, heterodox texts, and so forth), there emerged a system of professional scribes, a phenomenon in the history of sixteenth- and seventeenth-century Spain that remains very understudied, though it was of indubitable importance. These professional copyists received the name of *escritores* (writers), and many were also calligraphers or elementary schoolmasters, though many likewise developed a career as itinerant copyists serving private individuals, town councils, church chapters or the Crown itself.

To form an idea of their importance and the kind of assignments they received, let us consider the examples of two collections of letters and a diary that give ample testimony of what must have been a continuous movement of papers. Thus, the diary of Girolamo da Sommaia edited by Haley reveals that in Philip III's Salamanca there circulated in manuscript form such texts as "two handwritten volumes of Tacitus," some "couplets by Luis de Góngora," a Roman *gazzeta* (pieces of news from Italy in manuscript form), and "a letter from Antonio Pérez," the sort of documents that Da Sommaia was in the custom of having some penniless Basque students copy for him.[31] In Francisco of Portugal's correspondence between Madrid and Lisbon, together with numerous references to copies of his own compositions or of other authors who were triumphing in Philip IV's court in the mid-1620s, we find mention of a lady in the palace who has requested from him a copy of some chapters of *Belianís de Grecia* (*Belianis of Greece*), which the Portuguese nobleman was having copied and which, if indolence did not prevent it, he planned to augment with material added in his own hand.

In the correspondence between Lope de Vega and his patron the duke of Sessa we read the poet's announcement that he will be sending his *Soliloquios* (*Soliloquies*) in draft form; he asks that the duke "have it carefully copied and make certain the *escritor* does not lose those pages, because there are no other copies anywhere."[32] This was the same text that, in another letter from 1611, Lope found himself having to ask of a certain friar, even though he knew that in Madrid "everybody has a copy" and which the friar sent to him "under the condition that after having it copied, he would be certain to return the original."[33] Later, in August of 1617, Lope informs the duke that he had requested a copy of "a letter by Father Federico . . . and another, a discreet, prudent response to the first by the count of Los Arcos, who scolded the ecclesiastic rather much for his audacity."[34] In April 1619, the poet asks Sessa for a copy of the *Relazione* (*Report*) by the Venetian Simone Contarini, mentioning other copies of the same work that circulated at court, a text which in principle we would have expected to have been less accessible. Likewise, one would have imagined the *Instrucciones* (*Instructions*) written by Charles V for his son Philip II to have circulated only within the royal family's most intimate circle, but, on the contrary, as Woudhuysen has demonstrated, copies of the text even reached England, where Elizabeth Tudor herself owned a copy.

In the libraries of the court noblemen, it is common to find a series of miscellanea and volumes composed of various manuscripts, all of them simply the product of this accumulation of papers and copies that reflect the ever-changing political and cultural atmosphere which did not necessarily reach the printing press. Of course, these collections reveal their owners' bibliophilia—likewise associated with the possession of rare manuscripts—an interest exemplified by such figures as Astorga, Gondomar, Heliche, or Uceda. At the same time, however, aristocrats hired the services of professional scribes and men of letters also as a sign of distinction, in accordance with the commonplace that writing poorly was characteristic of the nobility.

Nonetheless, Alonso de Belvis Trejo, a writer from Toledo, published in 1678 his *Forma breve que se ha de tener en soltar o correr la mano en exercicio de escribir liberal* (*Brief Form in Which One Should Move One's Hand in the Free Exercise of Writing*), attacking Francisco de Quevedo because "he wrote that poor handwriting was a sign of nobility, but this is not true, for it is well known that there are many noblemen who write well and with style, and they are proud of their skill; those noblemen who do not do so meet the same fate as the rest of the Republic: because they have no practice, their writing is worse than when they were in school."[35] Let us now go hand in hand with Belvis Trejo to those schools where the Republic learns to write.

Chapter 4

Classrooms, Libraries, and Archives as the Culmination of Human Memory

Certain historians have insisted on presenting the eighteenth century as the century of pedagogy and the previous two hundred years as dominated by social discipline. Even without excluding justification for such a claim, one nonetheless cannot ignore the fact that the concept of discipline in and of itself reveals a concern for teaching and learning, as Álvaro Cavide indicates in his *Arte*, cited in Chapter 1, by defining man as that animal which is "disciplinable" ("able to be disciplined"), that is, the only one capable of learning and of being taught, from the cradle to the tomb.

One of the most curious metaphors about the human passage from earth to the heavens is to be found in Friar Diego de Silva y Pacheco's imprimatur for Juan de Santa María's *Dichoso fin* (*Fortunate End*), cited also in Chapter 1, when he mentions that upon setting his foot in heaven, Philip IV won an honorary *cátedra* (academic chair), an event which was of course celebrated with a celestial cheer. This "cátedra de inmortalidad" ("*cátedra* of immortality") was the consummation of the course of life, the lengthy school in which lettered men, I would add, would forge ahead from classroom to classroom, all the way from their primary studies to the university.

Though we should not forget the continuous, undeniable presence of oral and visual culture, as I have indicated already, writing became a principle characteristic of early modern civilization such that the practice came to be viewed as the consummation of humanity. In the mid-seventeenth century, Alonso González Bastones affirmed:

That man who does not know how to read, write and count, cannot be called a perfect man because these skills are the most necessary and useful remedy for nourishing oneself and surviving at any time and under any circumstances;

without them, man is not prepared for any occupation of brilliance, but only for vulgar and common jobs, and even these require that he be able to write, though this may be very little. And so, no one should scorn these skills, which should be made good use of, and therefore may these documents and words that Master Alonso González Bastones here offers with good will be held in high esteem.[1]

This splendid declaration is to be found in the text of an original sample of calligraphy today housed in the Museum of Pedagogy in Madrid, previously part of Rico y Sinobas's collection. With it, Master González Bastones sought to demonstrate the excellence of his own art and also to encourage potential students to join his school, in which—he promises—they would become "hombres completos" ("complete men").

The notion that a primary education was the beginning of a long path leading a man to moral perfection—not to mention his possible advancement by means of those "occupations of brilliance" referred to by González Bastones in his calligraphic sample—was a prevalent commonplace in the sixteenth and seventeenth centuries, whose principal propagandists were the schoolmasters themselves. Thus, Blas Antonio de Ceballos's *Libro histórico y moral*, cited in Chapter 1, carries the subtitle, "Perfecta instrucción para educar a la jubentud en virtud y letras" ("Perfect Instruction for the Education of Youths in Virtue and Letters").

Himself a schoolmaster with a school in Madrid near the Convent of the Mercedarians, Ceballos aimed in his book, finally, at nothing less than an affirmation of the nobility of his most liberal profession, just as painters, for example, had done already by seeking to transform themselves from mere artisans into artists. Thus, in its apology for elementary education, the *Libro histórico y moral* will make careful and devoted allusions to the numerous saints that "have served as teachers of the first rudiments,"[2] an indubitable indication of the superior qualities of Ceballos's profession. In addition, our author evokes what were then called *antigüedades del arte* (antiquities of art), by reporting on the mythical origins of the alphabet or on the first to cultivate letters, or even describing the legendary "inventors" of specific genres such as private correspondence, an honor he confers, as we have seen, upon none other than Túbal.

Furthermore, Ceballos offers us detailed information that today proves extraordinarily valuable in tracing the history of primary education in Hapsburg Spain. Especially deserving of our attention is not only his careful review of the great schoolmasters who had become famous from the time of Emperor Charles V (King Charles I of Spain) to that of Charles II, but also his discussion of the numerous treatises published during that century and a half, of schoolmasters' behavior in and out of school, and of their organization in confraternities, such as that of the Roman schoolmaster Saint Casiano, to which Ceballos himself belonged. If that were not enough, Ceballos manages to convey vivid scenes of daily life in primary schools, with advice on the devotional images that might decorate their walls, the thorny question of parents' visits, and the conflicts among the children: "one complains that his companions beat him; another that they call him names; another that they steal his ink; the fastidious one that they stain his paper and erase the page; and there is always one that tears to pieces the pages of the primers and other books with the styluses."[3] The schoolmasters themselves did not go unscathed, and would end up being "called names and made the object of burlesque songs."[4]

Ceballos, like González Bastones or Juan de Espinosa (mentioned in Chapter 3), had passed an exam in order to teach primary letters at court, and Alonso de Belvis Trejo (mentioned at the end of that chapter) was one of the examiners for such schoolmasters in Toledo and its district. Not everybody who taught elementary education, however, necessarily had passed an examination (a sample of handwriting demonstrating their mastery of the skill) to carry out this activity since, as Pedro Díaz Morante remarks in his *Segunda parte del arte de escribir* (*Second Part of the Art of Writing*), there were many that taught in secret, and even "some men who are left without a trade turn to teaching."[5] Certified schoolmasters approved by examination usually took in students as boarders, generally once they had reached six or seven years of age, and in a contract with the parents they promised to teach the child in two or three years how to read, to write—usually cursive and printing—and to count—that is, according to the five rules of "addition, subtraction, multiplication, whole division and fractions."[6]

Contracts with female teachers, though considerably less common, also survive, providing for the instruction of girls in reading, writing, sewing, and embroidery, though the opinion was widespread that women should not learn to write. Thus, the canon Pedro Sánchez in his *Árbol de consideración y varia doctrina* (*Tree of Consultation and Varied Teaching*), when delving into the matter regarding "the qualities a man should look for in the woman that will become his wife," proclaims with poorly concealed misogyny:

A man should seek a woman who does not know how to write, and even if she does not know how to read he should not turn her down because, since a woman should not own merchants' account books or manuals (even if her husband's manner and way of life requires them), nor should she take care of business, nor rent out the properties, nor receive payments from pensions or tributes, it is unnecessary for her to know how to write, for women should not follow the trade of public scribes, nor are they wise enough . . . to administer public offices.[7]

"She should pray devotedly with a rosary," continues the canon, "and if she knows how to read, she should read devotional books and books of good doctrine, for writing must be left to men. She should know how to use a needle well and how to use a spindle and distaff, having no need for the use of a pen."[8] This practice seems sadly to have been habitual among commoners, though some women were not condemned only to plying the needle, and some even managed to turn it into a pen. As extraordinary as she might have been for the period, it is worth mentioning the case of Cecília de Sa (or Deça) reported by Jerónimo Román in his *Segunda parte de las repúblicas del mundo* (*Second Part of the Republics of the World*), a woman who, "because her father prohibited her learning to write, by the letters she made in her embroideries and other needlework, managed to learn—so well that she can write whatever she wishes with great ease."[9]

In addition to the system of boarding schools with certified schoolmasters and the institution of private tutors for princes, young nobles, and sons of rich merchants, there also were primary schools dependent upon town councils, religious orders, and churches, where charitable donors often provided in their wills for the foundation of schools, which were always poorly funded and consequently without very qualified teachers. Finally, there are numerous testimonies that reading and writing was learned in the bosom of one's own family.

Though we know instructional methods existed that nowadays we would consider more modern and in which there could even be an element of play, elementary schooling was nonetheless based essentially on repetition, for both reading and writing. To learn to read, pupils repeated ABCs, syllabaries, and readings from primers, along with the most common prayers (thus linking elementary education closely to the teaching of religious doctrine, a connection Cátedra and Infantes have examined). It was also thought essential that, to learn to write, students should make repeated copies of samples of individual letters, then words and phrases, before going on to write texts in diverse styles of calligraphy on blank pages without tooling.

From these primary schools in the vernacular, students went on to learn Latin in the grammar schools, so numerous that they provoked from the beginning of the seventeenth century the suspicions of the so-called "biblioclastic" *arbitristas*, who argued in favor of closing many grammar schools in the belief they impeded productive activities.[10] What might be considered the most outstanding example of this attitude is the report titled *Por el agricoltura, criança, artífizes, marinería del Reyno. Contra el exceso de libros nuevos* (*In Defense of the Agriculture, Animal Husbandry, Manual Trades, and Maritime Activities of the Kingdom. Against the Excessive Number of New Books*), published anonymously in 1633, but thought to have been the work of Diego Hurtado de Mendoza, viscount of La Corzana, attacking both primary and grammar schools. In his opinion, the solution to the kingdom's decline was "to reduce the number of writing and grammar schools, in which the students (because of their schoolmasters' self-interest) are cheated and their time wasted, which they ought to spend learning trades that serve the common good."[11]

This *arbitrismo biblioclasta*, backed by various royal decrees against the proliferation of schools, above all those that were struggling financially in small towns, is a phenomenon that proves especially interesting for scholars today for the way it helps us understand what it meant to be literate in the sixteenth and seventeenth centuries. In

contrast to the contemporary notion that literacy for the moral perfection of the individual is a natural right, "biblioclasts" insisted that
knowing some Latin or simply learning to write meant the abandon-
ment of productive activities in favor of the lettered professions
(scribes, solicitors, jurists, and so on), which they considered harmful
given the allegedly excessive numbers of their practitioners. In short,
the biblioclasts—and also schoolmasters like González Bastones,
Ceballos, or the misogynist canon Sánchez—make it clear that literacy opened the way for change in the community and society in general. The author of *Por el agricoltura* thus insists that "the opportunity
for communication" by means of writing "inspires a great many men
to exile themselves from their homelands borne aloft by only the
wings of the plume and their books, removing them from the perse-
verance and virtue of work in their trades, upon which each and every
one is mutually dependent."[12]

Let us return, however, to the grammar schools. There, the students' basic studies were in Latin, along with some other subjects such
as rhetoric, philosophy, or mathematics and the unavoidable Christian doctrine, according to Kagan's admirable synthesis, which I follow here. Besides the typical schools of Latinity which were generally
under the authority of town councils (though some depended financially on charitable bequests and legacies), it is also worth highlight-
ing the Jesuits' interest in this level of education between the primary
schools and the universities, which we might suitably call "secondary
education."

In the grammar schools of the Jesuits we find a clear example of
social discipline of urban groups through education, which seems
to have paralleled the Society of Jesus's effort in their home missions. On the one hand, the Society showed an evident capacity for
innovation in their teaching methods with, for example, the inclu-
sion of theatrical pieces in instruction, similar to the ingenuity of the
missionaries (such as Father Jerónimo López) in their proselytiz-
ing *industrias*. On the other hand, the Jesuits used these schools to
indoctrinate the young in the renewed values of Catholic confessionalization, dedicating themselves especially to the sons of privileged
groups, who had to be modeled as perfect Catholics ready to support
or lead the Roman creed's reconquest of lost territories. As Kagan has
demonstrated, the Jesuits were especially interested in establishing

themselves in every major city, and by the beginning of the seventeenth century the Society had 118 schools in Spain.

The consummation of learning—and for the "biblioclasts" the ruin of the productive trades—was to be found at the universities, with their academic chairs, *colegios mayores* and *colegios menores*, bachelors, licenciates, and doctors, of which centers of higher learning there were more than thirty in 1600 in Spain.[13] From these institutions came many of the men who served the Hapsburg Crown, though they did not always escape the criticism of others from the very ranks of the learned, such as the professor from Alcalá, Alonso García de Matamoros, who affirms in his *Pro adserenda Hispanorum eruditione* (*For the Vindication of the Erudition of Spaniards*), "I do not yet understand by what evil fate the grave men of Salamanca and the first among their students so quickly aspire to the administration of the Republic and its honors—to govern everything as they please—with so much scorn for eloquence."[14]

Nonetheless, in no way can Master Matamoros be suspected of mistrusting letters; on the contrary, he considered them the way to reach "the summit of civility," against the opinion of those who imagined civility lay "in going about well-dressed and in not speaking Latin because it proves so very difficult."[15] This professor of rhetoric even proposes a model of the warrior king, who is at the same time wise, in imitation of the ancients, who "listened to the philosophers, read their books and meditated upon their precepts. What a beautiful sight, that of the warrior princes who argued cases in the Forum and disputed with philosophers in the schools!"[16] How far from ideal was, for instance, the profile of Philip III as a prince, who—though samples of his grammar exercises have survived—we know maintained that the study of letters "was not necessary or beneficial."[17] It was said of him in Portuguese, as if a proverb, "Little Prince Philip his Latin never learned."[18]

A proper understanding of written culture in sixteenth and seventeenth-century Spain cannot ignore this polemic, which also cannot be reduced to the mere cliché of arms versus letters. Rather, it can be viewed as a long-standing debate over what can be acquired through study and what is due simply to innate talent. In other words, we can observe in this dispute a meditation on the natural limits of art and science in such a delicate and important matter as determining

whether governing is a skill that can be learned or not, and consequently, with whom the prince should govern and from whom he
should seek advice.

In an evident sign of crude self-interest, some members of the aristocracy after 1550 came to insist that letters are only accessory, that
it is only the inborn virtues of the soul that authorize their status as
overlords. The age of such men as the marquis of Santillana (1398–
1458), in which noblemen had to prove themselves learned lest they
be considered fools, was now forgotten. Now no longer in confron-
tation with the clergy but with the *letrados* (lettered men) who had
obtained, and would continue to obtain, increasing influence over
the king, the nobility promoted as their ideal of civility a form of
ethics expressed in the figure of the innate courtier, with that curious
corollary that his handwriting should be poor as a sign of his caste.
In contrast, lettered men found their ideal of civility in the wisdom
bound up in written texts, acquired in the passage from classroom to
classroom, from the primary schools to the university colleges, and
stored away in libraries, which Manuel de Faria e Sousa called "bot-
tomless oceans" and which he claims he devoted himself to "navigat-
ing . . . with my little bark" for not less than forty years.[19]

Even the most obstinate critics of all that letters implied, both as
a profession and as a useful tool, could not ignore books in their triumph; nor did they, though it is important to stress that the majority
preferred books of literature or erudition (with these categories'
attendant ideological implications), seeking to become patrons of
famous authors or of academies or even to become poets themselves.
This desire is quite apparent, for instance, in the nobles who would
not refuse a dedication or who collected autograph copies of texts
and manuscript compilations of poetry and sage advice. It is likewise
apparent in collectors' glorying in the virtuosity with which they
assembled their libraries, just as it is apparent in the questionnaire
prepared for potential suitors of the count of Oropesa's daughter
alluded to at the beginning of Chapter 3, in which it will be recalled
that someone felt it necessary to include a question concerning "the
kinds of books and writing preferred" by the aspirant.

Note, however, that such behavior as this among the aristocracy can
also serve as a sign in its members of their inherently noble spirit: in
a liberal patron's magnanimity toward the learned men and literati;

in ownership of that rare and extraordinary text that reveals, at heart, the nature of whomever selected it. A good example of how the accumulation of books could be one more distinguished form of behavior among courtiers is the familiar image of the marquis of Heliche, a prominent figure in Philip IV's court, peevishly welcoming his numerous clients and petitioners from all over the kingdom in his grand and select library, with his rare and ancient codices bound in delicate red morocco leather. Indeed, in the sixteenth and seventeenth centuries one could find two extreme attitudes, clearly in conflict with each other, regarding the ownership of libraries. One perspective considered books inherently useful, while the other took them as just another sign in the rhetoric of distinction. Exemplifying the first attitude were the libraries of jurists, doctors, theologians, ecclesiastics, lettered men who served as political advisors, and members of numerous other occupations dependent on the knowledge of letters—collections encompassing the literate memory relative to their respective fields of specialization. The second attitude inspired the acquisition of what Cavallo has aptly called "books of the purple," a view of books apparent in the grandiose libraries assembled by certain nobles at court, which Frair Tomás Quixada, in his *Respuesta* (*Response*) to Villalba y Estañá, described with these witty verses:

I don't go searching in those libraries
owned by archbishops, dukes or by marquises,
for boasting's sake assembled, just for looks,
since rarely do their owners read their books.[20]

It goes without saying that these two attitudes about the significance of private libraries—whether of the sort owned by the socially eminent or those assembled for professional purposes—are rarely manifested in their extreme forms, unalloyed. Rather, it is much more common to encounter intermediate stances that view books simultaneously as instruments and as signs in and of themselves. Thus, one can move from a library assembled in artless imitation of aristocratic collections by a member of the *nouveau riche* or a new member of the nobility hoping to show off his newly acquired status through ownership of books, to the rich royal libraries, in which the rhetoric of social distinction reaches its majestic extreme, with extraordinary collections of ancient codices and rare works, but which also encompass all the knowledge conserved in writing that could serve as the basis for counseling the king.

The royal library at the monastery-palace of El Escorial is a good example of a treasury of books that inherently expresses Philip II's majesty, by virtue of the high quality of its original copies. At the same time, however, it can also be understood as an almost immeasurable deposit of universal knowledge, in the service of this Catholic monarch's confessional objectives. Something similar may be said of aristocratic libraries whose owners mixed their "books of the purple" with books useful for governing, either in imitation of the royal model, or because, out of conviction or necessity, they decided to round off their character (which they never renounced as a mark of social difference) with the teachings to be found in certain choice texts.

A curious episode in the courtly career of Luis Fernández de Córdoba, duke of Sessa, studied by González de Amezúa in his edition of the correspondence between Lope de Vega and the duke, can help illuminate this last point. Several letters in the duke's correspondence from 1619 and 1620 pertain precisely to his intention to acquire some "legajos de papeles" ("bundles of documents") in manuscript copy that the influential protonotary of Aragon, Francisco Gassol, had owned, as well as "dos papeles" ("two documents") that Sessa hoped to have composed by none other than the Jesuit humanist historian Juan de Mariana. One of these latter two documents would explain "the way in which a man of my quality should hold himself if he were to obtain his prince's good favor," alluding to the position of influence Sessa then sought in the court, while the other would discuss "the way in which a lord can successfully govern in his estates," since the duke's were "so far apart from each other and some so close to estates owned by other powerful men, that I think one would have to carry the sun in his hands to see such dark difficulties and discern them clearly."[21]

Sessa admits in a letter to Eugenio Narbona that the majority of his fellow aristocrats would consider it useless to read a document on the government of vassals (such as the one he was requesting from Father Mariana) because "they think nothing more falls to the lot of the proprietor than the fruits of his estates."[22] Nonetheless, the Duke insisted on acquiring these guides to aristocratic behavior in manuscript copies since, as he explains in a letter to Andrés de Rozas regarding Gassoil's papers, in them "one can follow the path of practice with easier and more certain understanding,"[23] claiming incidentally that one could not find in common printed books such a practical path.

Either simply for the sake of ostentation (as González de Amezúa affirms), or out of prudence à la Justus Lipsius or Tacitus, Sessa insists on the need to read manuscripts that advise on matters of state or on matters of one's own estates. Furthermore, it is important to stress that while Mariana could offer the authorized teachings Sessa claims he could not find in the library his father, Antonio Folch de Cardona, had bequeathed him, Gassol's documents would serve to swell his archives, a depository of writing no less important than a collection of books for a nobleman with aspirations to influence in government and court.

In a letter to Father Hortensio Félix de Paravicino, whose help he requested to have Gassol's papers sent from Valladolid, Sessa explains how he hoped the bundles of papers, which "are dead, and nothing can revive them," could nonetheless be of practical use.[24] He points out that "their subject matter by chance applies to those of us not far from positions of responsibility in governments, and I am anxious to sift through them since this class of manuscripts does no harm to those of us who lead the active life."[25]

For some strange reason, the building of archives is one of the forgotten areas in the history of written culture in sixteenth- and seventeenth-century Spain. The maintenance of royal, aristocratic, municipal, and ecclesiastic archives is hardly mentioned, as is the creation of important new archives such as the collections at Simancas or at the embassy in Rome, and when they are discussed, it is always in the context of the increasing use of writing as an instrument of power, as I have discussed in Chapter 3. Without a doubt, the strengthening of the archives serving the Crown and other jurisdictions warrants the greatest attention. At the same time, however, we should not neglect the emergence of small private archives, which gathered together little more than property titles, testaments or letters patent of entailment; nor should we forget that the nobility strove to enrich their own archives with clearly political objectives. In this light, the duke of Sessa's insistence on obtaining Gassol's "dead papers" in 1619, with the aim of sifting through them since there was presumably much he could learn there, is in no way exceptional at a time when the great personages at the courts of Philip II and Philip III sought after such archives as if they were a veritable political gold mine.

A good example of aristocrats' interest in such collections are the transformations undergone by the archive we know today as the Fondo de Altamira, in which the papers of Diego de Espinosa, Mateo Vázquez de Lecca, Luis de Requeséns, and Juan de Zúñiga, among many others, were accumulated, having circulated from hand to hand until they reached the Houses of Velada and Astorga, and from there, through marriages, to the House of Altamira. To confirm court politicians' interest in archival papers, however, we need only turn to what is perhaps the most widely known case, namely, the royal letters patent of 1625 and 1632 by which the king's favorite, the count-duke of Olivares, obtained the entail of "many books and papers that were scattered in different places . . . most of them pertaining to grave and important matters from the time of Emperor Charles V, my great-grandfather, and of my lords the kings, my grandfather and father (God rest their souls), and some of them being original copies."[26]

Private individuals' efforts at acquiring small archives can be considered the most eloquent sign of the desire to possess what we might call the written memory of Monarchy—manifested, therefore, not only in royal archives, such as those of Simancas or the Crown of Aragon. It was here, however, that the most substantial collections of documents were accumulated. According to Rodríguez de Diego's study, the fame of the archive installed in the fortress at Simancas spread until it came to be identified with the memory of the institution of the monarchy itself and, what is more, as a symbol of the memory of the past in general, to which numerous individuals and groups would come in search of documents as proof of rights or obligations.

In light of my assertion at the end of Chapter 2 that it is possible to view the proverb "Hablen cartas, callen barbas" ("Let letters speak, from whiskers not a squeak") as exemplifying the mark left by writing on Golden Age culture, it will be understood why archives became the symbol of the will to make human deeds, ideas and sentiments lasting. Alonso de Ovalle, mentioned in Chapter 1, in his *Histórica relación del*

Reyno de Chile, found that a crucial difference between Andean cultures without writing and European cultures was that the former had no archives and, consequently, had no memory of the most ancient things that "other nations" had deposited in archives "for the memory of posterity."[27] Let us recall, however, that the Jesuit father harbored no doubts that those cultures had devised the best way to remember their own history and traditions, by means of certain individuals responsible for repeating them to the sound of a drum on holy days. Indeed, Ovalle insightfully records that "this Indian was the archivist, or, rather, the archive of that people."[28] Where there was humanity, there memory would be, and the archive could be viewed as the culmination of human memory conserved in writing.

Up to this point, it should be noted, I have referred mainly to libraries and archives, that is, to books and documents that form a more or less organized collection, preserved until their owner's death and in many cases, associated thereafter with his heirs or some institution charged with its conservation. I have already had occasion to show, however, how the daily relationship with written texts was widespread in the sixteenth and seventeenth centuries, as can be observed in such phenomena as viva-voce readings, the lending or rental of books, the familiarity among the illiterate with written documents, the profusion of signs and inscriptions in streets and squares, or publishers' efforts to satisfy popular demand in the book market. Furthermore, there exist numerous testimonies of texts produced for amusement (novellas, songs, plays, chapbooks, and so forth) or for special occasions and uses (school primers with orthographic and calligraphic rules, prayers, reports, brief documents of a few pages, and so forth)—texts that would not become part of lasting collections because they were spent and disposed of as soon as their purpose was satisfied.

In these pages I have sought to adopt a perspective that takes into account this pragmatic use of texts, which could exhaust the reading of a book at the very moment it is being consumed and enjoyed. From this eminently practical point of view, the differences between hearing, seeing, and reading or writing are considerably reduced because the culture of sixteenth- and seventeenth-century Spain resorted to oral persuasion as often as visual representations of ideas and sentiments or their dissemination via writing in a publishing market in which the borders between literate and illiterate culture became blurred. Sixteenth- and seventeenth-century culture did this on its own, by taking full advantage of sermons, songs, engravings, printed books or manuscript copies, reading some texts out loud and others in silence, mixing images and texts with voices that spoke with fright, fury or kindness.

In 1555, Juan de Angulo published a curious book entitled *Flor de solemnes alegrías* (*The Most Select of Solemn Gaieties*) in which he gives a detailed account of "the festivities in the imperial city of Toledo in celebration of the conversion of the Kingdom of England" under the government of Mary Tudor.[29] The description allows us to imagine a typical public festivity of the sixteenth and seventeenth centuries: sermons and prayers, a garrulous mass of people who have risen early to secure a prominent post from which to observe the processions, long parades of local associations (guilds, confraternities, and so forth), carts that travel along the streets carrying allegorical representations painted in bright colors. It is owing to a printed book that we have an account of that oral and visual effusion, but writing itself also was an integral component of the celebration.

One of the carts in the parade belonged to the officials of the Holy Inquisition in the city. A richly adorned horse pulled this cart on which they had placed a great serpent and an armed knight seated astride it, symbolizing the victory of the *miles Christi* over heresy in England. This knight, though a polished expression of visual culture, was nonetheless tossing into the enthusiastic crowd "little papers with this poem written on them":

Here let the serpent so unruly
of humans' base carnality
before the Truth his neck bow duly,
his cart pull with humility.[30]

Around the same time, the Shrovetide celebration at Toledo filled the streets with masks, as reported in minute detail in a *Memorial de la rreductión de Inglaterra al gremio o unión de la sancta madre Iglesia* (*Account of the Return of England to the Company or Union of the Holy Mother Church*).[31] There were masks of every sort: Moors, Jews, university doctors, physicians, savages, madmen, pastry makers, cuckolds, pilgrims, messengers, African men and women, Portuguese, nuns, widows, Amazons, Basque women, kings, shepherds, hermits, and even monks. It is the masks of "Celestinas with their scar and little baskets of perfume," however, that demonstrate how the importance of writing and authors would continue to grow in the mentality of Spaniards of the Golden Age, and it is with this image that I will conclude.[32] Writing had begun to dominate the imagination of even the popular masses in their disguises.

Notes

Foreword

1. Fernando Bouza, *Del escribano a la biblioteca: La civilización escrita europea en la alta Edad Moderna (siglos XV–XVII)* (Madrid: Síntesis, 1992) and *Imagen y propaganda: Capítulos de historia cultural del reinado de Felipe II* (Madrid: Akal, 1998).

2. The work of Armando Petrucci is essential here, of which *Writers and Readers in Medieval Italy: Studies in the History of Written Culture* (New Haven, Conn.: Yale University Press, 1995) and *Writing the Dead: Death and Writing Strategies in the Western Tradition* (Stanford, Calif.: Stanford University Press, 1998) are available in English.

3. See Roger Chartier, "Culture écrite et littérature à l'âge moderne," *Annales: Histoire, Sciences Sociales* 56 (July–October 2001): 783–802.

4. Ann Rosalind Jones and Peter Stallybrass, *Renaissance Clothing and the Materials of Memory* (Cambridge: Cambridge University Press, 2000), 134–71.

5. See James Amelang, *The Flight of Icarus: Artisan Autobiography in Early Modern Europe* (Stanford Calif., Stanford University Press, 1998); Antonio Castillo Gómez, *Escrituras y escribientes: Prácticas de la cultura escrita en una ciudad del Renaciemiento* (Las Palmas: Fundación de Enseñanza Superior a Distancia de Las Palmas de Gran Canaria, 1997), and "Entre public et privé: Stratégies de l'écrit dans l'Espagne du Siècle d'Or," *Annales: Histoire, Sciences Sociales* 56 (July–October 2001): 803–29.

6. For Italy, see Armando Petrucci, *Public Lettering: Script, Power, and Culture* (Chicago: University of Chicago Press, 1993); Laura Antonucci, "La scrittura giudicata: Perizie grafiche in procesi romani del primo Seicento," *Scrittura e Civiltà* 13 (1989): 489–534; and Claudia Evangelisti, "'Libelli famosi' processi per scritte infamanti nella Bologna di fine '500," *Annali della Fondazione Einaudi* 27 (1992): 181–239. For England, see Juliet Fleming, *Graffiti and the Writing Arts of Early Modern England* (Philadelphia: University of Pennsylvania Press, 2001). For Spain, see Antonio Castillo Gómez, "'Amanecieron

en todas las partes públicas . . . ': Un viaje al país de las denuncias," in *Escribir y leer en el siglo de Cervantes*, ed. Antonio Castillo Gómez (Barcelona: Gedisa, 1999), 143–91.

7. On the *pliegos sueltos*, the fundamental studies are those of María Cruz García de Enterría, *Sociedad y poesía de cordel en el Barroco* (Madrid: Taurus, 1973); Victor Infantes, "Los pliegos sueltos poéticos: Constitución tipográfica y contenido literario (1482–1600)," in Infantes, *En el Siglo de Oro: Estudios y textos de literatura aurea* (Potomac, Md., Scripta Humanistica, 1992), 47–52, and Pedro Cátedra, *Invención, difusión y recepción de la literatura popular impresa (siglo XVI)* (Mérida: Editora Regional de Extremadura, 2002).

8. For England, see Tessa Watt, *Cheap Print and Popular Piety, 1550–1640* (Cambridge: Cambridge University Press, 1991); Adam Fox, "Ballads, Libels, and Popular Ridicule in Jacobean England," *Past and Present* 145 (1994): 47–83, and *Oral and Literate Culture in England, 1500–1700* (Oxford: Clarendon Press, 2000); Margaret Spufford, *Small Books and Pleasant Histories: Popular Fiction and Its Readership in Seventeenth-Century England* (London: Methuen, 1981); for France, see Roger Chartier, *The Cultural Uses of Print in Early Modern France* (Princeton, N.J.: Princeton University Press, 1987). For a comparative perspective, see Roger Chartier and Hans-Jürgen Lüsebrink, eds., *Colportage et lecture populaire: Imprimés de large circulation en Europe XVIe–XIXe siècles* (Paris: IMEC Editions et Editions de la Maison des Sciences de l'Homme, 1996).

9. See Margit Frenk, *Entre la voz y el silencio* (Alcalá de Henares: Centro de Estudios Cervantinos, 1977) and María Cruz García de Enterría, "Lecturas y rasgos de un público," *Edad de Oro* 12 (1993): 119–30.

10. Elizabeth Eisenstein, *The Printing Press as an Agent of Change: Communications and Cultural Transformations in Early Modern Europe*, 2 vols. (Cambridge: Cambridge University Press, 1979) and *The Printing Revolution in Early Modern Europe* (Cambridge: Cambridge University Press, 1993).

11. Fernando Bouza, "¿Para que imprimir? De autores, público, impresores, y manuscritos en el Siglo de Oro," *Cuadernos de Historia Moderna* (Madrid) 18 (1997): 31–50.

12. Fernando Bouza, *Corre manuscrito: Una historia cultural del Siglo de Oro* (Madrid: Marcial Pons, 2001).

13. See Harold Love, *Scribal Publication in Seventeenth-Century England* (Oxford: Clarendon Press, 1993), reissued as *The Culture and Commerce of Texts: Scribal Publication in Seventeenth-Century England* (Amherst: University of Massachusetts Press, 1998); Arthur F. Marotti, *Manuscript, Print, and the English Renaissance Lyric* (Ithaca, N.Y., Cornell University Press, 1995), and H. R. Woudhuysen, *Sir Philip Sidney and the Circulation of Manuscripts, 1558–1640* (Oxford: Clarendon Press, 1996).

14. Ann Blair, "Humanist Methods in Natural Philosophy: The Commonplace Book," *Journal of the History of Ideas* 53 (1992): 541–51; Lisa Jardine and Anthony Grafton, "'Studied for Action': How Gabriel Harvey Read His Livy," *Past and Present* 129 (1990): 30–78; and Francis Goyet, *Le sublime du "lieu commun": L'invention rhétorique à la Renaissance* (Paris: Honoré Champion, 1996).

15. Ann Moss, *Printed Commonplace-Books and the Structuring of Renaissance Thought* (Oxford: Clarendon Press, 1996).

16. Fernando Bouza has dedicated numerous studies to court culture and aristocratic practices. See, among others, his *Locos, enanos y hombres de placer en la corte de los Austrias* (Madrid: Temas de Hoy, 1991, 1996), his recent *Palabra e imagen en la Corte: Cultura oral y visual de la nobleza en al Siglo de Oro* (Madrid: Abada Editores, 2003) and his essay, "Corte es decepción: Don Juan de Silva, conde de Portalegre," in *La corte de Felipe II*, ed. José Martínez Millán (Madrid: Alianza Editorial, 1994), 451–502. He also contributed a chapter to this book on "La majestad de Felipe II: Construcción del mito real," 37–72.

17. For studies or reflections in a similar vein, see Natalie Zemon Davis, *Society and Culture in Early Modern France* (Stanford, Calif.: Stanford University Press, 1975); Carlo Ginzburg, *The Cheese and the Worms: The Cosmos of a Sixteenth-Century Miller* (Baltimore: Johns Hopkins University Press, 1980); Michel de Certeau, *The Practice of Everyday Life*, trans. Steven Rendall (Berkeley: University of California Press, 1984); and Claude Grignon and Jean-Claude Passeron, *Le savant et le populaire: Misérabilisme et populisme en sociologie et en littérature* (Paris: Gallimard / Seuil, 1989).

18. The studies Bouza has dedicated to Portugal in the sixteenth and seventeenth centuries, especially during the period of Spanish domination, have been gathered together in *Portugal no tempo dos Felipes: Política, cultura, representações (1580–1668)* (Lisbon: Cosmos, 2000).

19. See Donald F. McKenzie, "Speech-Manuscript-Print," in *New Directions in Textual Studies*, ed. Dave Oliphant and Robin Bradford (Austin: Harry Ransom Humanities Research Center, 1990), 86–109, reprinted in McKenzie, *Making Meaning: "Printers of the Mind" and Other Essays*, ed. Peter D. McDonald and Michael F. Suarez, S.J. (Amherst, Mass.: University of Massachusetts Press, 2002), 237–58. One should note that Bouza's Spanish translation of McKenzie's *Bibliography and the Sociology of Texts* (Cambridge: Cambridge University Press, 1999) is currently in press.

20. Louis Marin, "Lire un tableau: Une lettre de Poussin en 1639," in *Pratiques de la lecture*, ed. Roger Chartier (Marseille: Rivages, 1985), 102–24; also Marin, *Des pouvoirs de l'image: Gloses* (Paris: Seuil, 1993), 72–101.

21. Among other examples, see the books by Manuel Peña Díaz, *El laberinto de los libros: Historia cultural de la Barcelona del Quinientos* (Madrid: Fundación Sánchez Ruipérez, 1997) and *Cataluña en el Renacimiento: Libros y lenguas (Barcelona, 1473–1600)* (Lleida: Editorial Milenio, 1996); Carlos Alberto González Sánchez, *Los mundos del libro: Medios de difusión de la cultura occidental en las Indias de los siglos XVI y XVII* (Seville: Universidad de Sevilla, 1999), Javier Antón Pelayo, *La herencia cultural: Alfabetización y lectura en la ciudad de Girona (1747–1807)* (Bellaterra: Universidad Autónoma de Barcelona, 1998); and José Pardo Tomás, *Ciencia y censura: La Inquisición española y los libros científicos en los siglos XVI y XVII* (Madrid: Consejo Superior de Investigaciones Científicas, 1991).

Chapter 1. Hearing, Seeing, Reading, and Writing: The Forms and Uses of Words, Images, and Writing

1. "Brava cosa es la crueldad con que el tiempo lo consume todo, pues no basta contra él armadura fuerte ni muros de metal," *Discurso de la comparación de la antigua y moderna pintura y escultura* (*Discourse on the Comparison of Ancient and Modern Painting and Sculpture*), ms. 19639, Biblioteca Nacional, Madrid, fol. 86v.

2. "Con una espada de pluma / y un escudo de papel."

3. "Se inventó para ayuda y reparo de la memoria."

4. "La memoria sólo cobra fuerças todas las veces que torna a leer lo que ya desfallecía y se yva olvidando."

5. "Archivo de aquel pueblo"; "para mantener la memoria de lo succedido en él desde el diluvio era obligado a repetirlo todos los días de fiesta al son del tanbor, y cantando como lo hazía en aquel lugar, y para que esta memoria no faltasse jamás tenía obligación de ir industriando a otros, que después de sus días le succediessen en este officio."

6. "Con una espada de pluma / y un escudo de papel / haré quel tiempo cruel / una tilde no consuma / de las proezas de aquél."

7. "Sólo él estudia y aprende y naturalmente desea saber más," chapter 27, ms. 2843, Biblioteca Nacional, Madrid.

8. "Para saber de sus parientes, y amigos que poblavan otras provincias."

9. "Éstas fueron las primeras que se usaron en el mundo, que bien consideradas son una conversación particular, un instrumento con que se da a entender el conçepto de los coraçones, y la pluma viene a ser un sexto sentido para los ausentes y una respiración que alienta el ánimo, de la manera que un retrato recrea la vista."

10. "Un retrato en acto de la habla e una fama de las palabras que queda después que as hablado o una imagen o vida que *inmediate* que la vees te traerá a la memoria lo que representa, como el pintor que pinta la figura que quien fácilmente se conoce por ella."

11. "No sé quién decía que las cartas son oración mental a los ausentes y decía bien porque mientras se escriue se piensa en el sujeto a quien se escriue, se habla con él en el entendimiento, en quien se representa al viuo su ymagen." The duke's correspondence has been edited by Agustín González de Amezúa in the same volume dedicated to Lope de Vega's: Lope de Vega Carpio, *Epistolario de Lope de Vega* (Madrid: Real Academia Española, 1989).

12. "Aquél que de leer tiene más uso / de ver letreros sólo está confuso."

13. "Un famoso tudesco de Maguncia / en quien la Fama su valor renuncia."

14. "Sin ella muchos siglos se han pasado / y no vemos que en este se levante / un Jerónimo santo, un Augustino."

15. "Superfluidad y demasías."

16. "Prohivir luego del todo la licençia de escribir en esta facultad y que de fuera no entrasen más libros della ni de los que están escritos ni de los que de nuevo se escriviere." Ms. 17787, Biblioteca Nacional, Madrid.

17. "Hasta Christo tuvo su conveniencia en que no huviesse papel y tinta en su execución, porque a lo menos no pago costas"; "aora [mundo] estáis más empapelado, mas no por eso más bien aconsejado." "Sermón del Viernes Sexto de Quaresma. Predicado en la Capilla Real. Año de 1662" ("Sermon for the Sixth Friday of Lent, Delivered in the Royal Chapel in 1662"), in Vieira, *Sermones* (Barcelona, 1685).

18. "La cosa mesma y también el mesmo concepto"; "vozes o palabras"; "comunicar a los que assiten presentes los conceptos del ánimo"; "a los caracteres, letras o figuras para declarar a los ausentes nuestros designios, pensamientos y afectos, o para introduzirnos en el conocimiento del tercero."

19. "el leer es para percibir"; "el mirar una figura introduze en la mesma inteligencia."

20. "Que si [los padres] no son vascongados de ninguna manera serán a propósito para la enseñança de la doctrina porque casi todos no entienden romançe ni más que su vascuence." Pedro Portocarrero, *Carta familiar del Obispo de Calahorra, Pedro Portocarrero, sobre las misiones de interior* (*Familiar Letter from the Bishop of Calahorra, Pedro Portocarrero, Regarding Home Missions,* Logroño, 1593), Patronato Eclesiástico, 40, Archivo General, Simancas.

21. Martín de la Naja, *El missionero perfecto* (Saragossa, 1678)

22. "Saque poco a poco el retrato del alma condenada"; "arrima el retrato y saca el Santo Christo."

23. "En Sermón de Passión alquiló un bastage y lo mostró al pueblo medio desnudo y salpicado de almagre, en vez de Ecce Homo."

24. "Catecismo y axiomas doctrinales para labradores y gente sencilla."

25. Respeta mucho a los reyes / y obedece bien sus leyes. / La República es perdida / si anda sin esta medida. / En faltándole esta concordia / todo se abrasa en discordia. / Si el rey fuese despreciado / el reino ya está acabado. / Si el Rey no es obedecido / el Reino ya está perdido. / Sin respeto al magistrado / el pueblo es desbaratado."

26. "Se hizo pintar cuadros del suceso."

27. "Estas pinturas sobre el rumor antecedente, sirvieron de nuevas lenguas y testigos mudos." *Memorial sobre las razones por las que no se debe imprimir la Historia que trata de la guerra de Pernambuco por Duarte de Albuquerque* (*Report Regarding the Reasons Duarte de Albuquerque's History of the War of Pernambuco Should Not Be Printed,* c. 1644), ms. Add. 28401, British Library, London.

Chapter 2. The Persuasion of the Word: A Voice; The Wonder of Images: A Portrait; The Power of Writing: A Talisman

1. "Tenía la voz clara y muy apacible." For this and the following references to Francisco Hurtado de Mendoza, see my "Docto y devoto: La biblioteca del Marqués de Almazán y Conde de Monteagudo (Madrid, 1591)," in *Hispania-Austria II: Die Epoche Philipps II (1556–1598),* ed. Friedrich Edelmayer,

Studien zur Geschichte und Kultur der iberischen und iberoamerikanischen Länder 5 (Munich: R. Oldenbourg, 1999), 247–310.

2. The original makes fun of an Andalusian accent by exaggerating a typical feature, which might have sounded like a lisp to Castilians, effected in this passage not only by the arbitrary substitution of *s* by *z*, *ç*, or *c* before *e* and *i* (representing the interdental fricative of standard Castilian, somewhat like the English *th*) but also by the selection of words that begin with that sound ordinarily, thus producing a generally nonsensical tirade. This translation attempts to produce a similar effect in English with an exaggerated rendering of syllable-final *r*, etc., in a stereotype of an accent from the Southern United States. The original passage, with translation, is as follows: "Çierto que uzé ez pulidicimo en çuz coçaz y le devo tanto que no me çabré explicar. Cepa que a todos los gatoz que me embizten con ezta priça, loz digo zape, y azí contentaré con eza fineza y coma de aquí adelante çorraz, çernícaloz y çigüeñaz, beba çupia o çumanque, tome cebadilla, cúreze con centaura eza locura que le atoziga y zi quiere divertirse bayle la zarabanda que ez un çambacañuto y no mereze máz rezpuesta çu atrevimiento" ("Forsooth, sir, your manners are very polished, and I am so beholden to you that words fail me. Know that to every cat that assails me so hastily, I say, 'Scat!' and I'll pay you that very compliment. From now on, eat vixens, kestrels and storks, drink silty or cheap wine, take wild rye, cure yourself with centaury of that madness that plagues you, and if you want to have fun, dance a saraband, for you're just a glutton, and your boldness deserves no further answer than this.") Translators' note.

3. "Honbre de pocas palabras y essas graues y muy consideradas y esto reconoçe fácilmente quien le oye hablar," *Algunos hechos famosos y genealogía de la Casa de los Gonzaga* (*Various Famous Deeds and the Genealogy of the House of Gonzaga*), ms. M 5, Biblioteca Universitaria, Valencia.

4. "Muita graça no falar"; "não lhe fora possível dissimular quem era." Quoted in Carlos A. Ferreira, "D. Francisco de Portugal: Elementos para su bio-bibliografía," *Biblos* 22 (1946): 607–73.

5. "Por qué no hablava castellano"; "siempre catalan"; "que por no mentir." Antonio Agustín, *Alveolus*, edited and translated by Cándido Flores Sellés, Clásicos Olvidados 6 (Madrid: Fundación Universitaria Española, 1982), 143.

6. "Quinto elemento de corte." *Intruçiones de reglas de Juan de Vega con el comento de Dom Francisco Rolim senhor de las vilhas de Azambuja, Monteargil y Marmelar* (*Rulebook of Juan de Vega, with the Commentary of Sir Francisco Rolim, Lord of the Towns of Azambuja, Monteargil and Marmelar*), ms. 51-II-42, no. 41, Biblioteca da Ajuda, Lisbon, fol.70v.

7. "Dezir a nadie lástima ni cosa que le pese." I cite the *Instrucción* by Juan de Vega expanded upon by the count of Portalegre and Peranda's *Instrucción* according to my edition in "Cinco piezas para una práctica nobiliaria de la corte," appendix to *Capítulos de historia cultural del reinado de Felipe II* (Madrid: Akal, 1998).

8. "Algunos piensan que con las mugeres no se han de hablar sino gentilezas y dulçuras y por esto se embaraçan algunas vezes de llegarlas a

hablar se ha de advertir que con ellas en especial quanto más principales se ha de hablar lo mismo que con los hombres, cómo será, cómo dormistes esta noche, o llegastes cansada, o qué os parece desta tierra, o desta casa, y cosas desta qualidad."

9. "Con cortar el razonamiento o saltar en otro. Mas esto o no suzede vien o no vasta siempre. Otros dizen que no saben y esto es gran herror, porque niegan la verdad y dizen lo que no es." "Instrucción de Pietro Gaetano cuando fue a servir a Alejandro Farnesio, Príncipe de Parma" ("Guide for Pietro Gaetano When He Went to Serve Alessandro Farnese, Prince of Parma"), in Fernando Bouza, *Imagen y propaganda: Capítulos de historia cultural del reinado de Felipe II.* Akal Universitaria, Serie Historia Moderna 200 (Madrid: Akal, 1998), 235–45.

10. "Beata Santa Anastasia, en medio de la mar una casa tenía, ni ella se bañaba ni al fondo se iba, mas por tu santidad y virginidad me digas la vía de la verdad de lo que te quiero preguntar"; "el dicho conjuro, el cual había de ir diciendo la dicha tal criatura que había que llamar a quien quería que viniese."

11. "Sobre ser clara, era tan flexible y acomodada su voz que exprimía con ella variedad de afectos fácilmente, porque en los passos de enseñança era agradable, en los de reprehensión terrible; en los de exortación, blanda; en los coloquios, tierna y devota. Finalmente, con el trueno formidable de su voz, atemorizava los coraçones de los pecadores y con el rayo ardiente de sus palabras los ería y penetrava."

12. "Ciento y tantas oraciones"; "un tono bajo, reposado y muy sonable que hacía resonar la iglesia donde rezaba."

13. "No hay tiro de artillería / como el hablar indecente; / al que hablare torpemente / gritemos 'Ave María'."

14. "Caracteres . . . para declarar a los ausentes nuestros designios, pensamientos y afectos."

15. *Memorial informatorio por los pintores.* Published in *Diálogos de la pintura: su defensa, origen, essencia, definición, modos y diferencias, al gran monarcha de las Españas y Nuevo Mundo, don Felipe IIII*, by Vicente Carducho (Madrid: Francisco Martínez, 1633).

16. "Por onde o coração recebe o amor"; "per onde os amigos ausentes comunicam seus conceitos e mostram a verdadeira fé de seus ânimos." "Carta curiosa escrita do Autor a um grande seu amigo" ("Curious Letter Written by the Author to a Great Friend of His"), quoted according to Andrée Rocha, *A epistolografia em Portugal* (Lisbon: Imprensa Nacional-Casa da Moeda, 1985), 125.

17. Diego de la Torre, *Memorial figurado enviado por Diego de la Torre a Felipe II* (*Illustrated Report Sent by Diego de la Torre to Philip II* (Tunja, 1584). Mapas, Planos y Dibujos XXVI-60, Archivo General, Simancas.

18. "La pintura hace poderosa impresión en los ánimos"; "Por eso los que procuraban hacer odioso a los pueblos a Atila, rey de los hunnos, que venía asolando a Europa, lo pintaban con cuernos; los hereges pintan algunas dignidades católicas en forma horrible para engañar a los rústicos; los

portugueses, en las guerras del rey don Juan I, con Castilla, pintaron en las banderas al infante don Juan (que era muy amado) medio hermano del mismo rey, preso como lo tenían los castellanos y con cadenas." I quote according to the seventeenth-century Castilian translation by Diego Suárez de Figueroa in the edition published in Murcia in 1882 (338).

19. "Dibuxo de una persona monstruosa"; "porque no llegue agora a noticia de la rreyna que no es bueno en este tiempo." Autograph note by Philip II in *Carta de Vespasiano Gonzaga a Mateo Vázquez de Lecca remitiendo el dibujo de una persona monstruosa* (*Letter from Vespasiano Gonzaga to Mateo Vázquez de Lecca accompanying a drawing of a monstrous person*), Valencia, 21 de octubre de 1571[?], Instituto Valencia de Don Juan, Madrid.

20. "Stupidi alla presenza della real Maestá di Filippo secondo."

21. "El semblante, aora compuesto, aora sereno, aora nublado, imite al cielo que con el variar de aspectos se ve mostrar la diferencia de los tiempos"; "es prudencia grande servirse de los ojos por lengua."

22. "A un tiempo presente en todos sus estados, causando alegría"; "amor e respeto."

23. "Un estudiante latino en la faltriguera para que cuando le ubiera menester me dijera todo lo que yo quería."

24. "Ciertas estampas que suelen yntitular en Italia *il mondo alla roversa.*" *Relación enviada a Felipe II sobre las jurisdicciones de Milán y conflictos con el Arzobispo Borromeo* (*Report Sent to Philip II Regarding the Administrative Districts of Milán and the Conflicts with Archbishop Borromeo*, c. 1595), ms. 12851, Biblioteca Nacional, Madrid.

25. "El bassallo juzga y el rey es juzgado, el cavallo es cochero y el cochero tira de la carroça."

26. "Los muchachos que por carnestolendas, con un poco de azafrán y de almagre, pintan unos gallos para poner en sus reguileros"; "aún les parecerá que serán capaces de poder cantar." I quote according to Emilio Casares, "Espina, Juan de," in *Biografías y documentos sobre música y músicos españoles* by Francisco Asenjo Barbieri, ed. Casares, Legado Barbieri 1 (Madrid: Fundación Banco Exterior, 1986).

27. "Porque nosotros pintamos sólo con natural a lo que hicieron los grandes hombres con grande estudio."

28. "En chemise"; "mal advise"; "jeux et putains." Sara T. Nalle, *God in La Mancha: Religious Reform and the People of Cuenca, 1500–1650* (Baltimore: Johns Hopkins University Press, 1992), 153, plate 6.

29. *Memoriales y cartas presentadas al concilio provincial de Salamanca* (*Reports and Letters Presented to the Provincial Council of Salamanca*, 1566), Casa de Cadaval, maço 17, Arquivo Nacional da Torre do Tombo, Lisbon, fol. 8r. The technique of *estofado* was developed specifically in Spain and involved coating a wooden statue or altarpiece with a layer of plaster, then gilding the entire piece or a large portion of it. Paint was applied over the gilding, and subsequently scraped away where the artist wished to reveal the gold underneath in, for example, an ornate pattern. Translators' note.

30. "Donde están pintadas santas ystorias de la sagrada scriptura"; "en tales lugares no son rreberençiadas, mas antes se rríen."

31. "Por yr mal pintadas no ponen devoçión."

32. "A qualquier impresor de qualquiera obispado pueda ynprimir qualesquier libros de officios y bien de la república que son neçessarios para el común, como sean vistos y examinados, porque ay muchos libros de cantería, de carpintería, de entalladores y pintores, plateros, freneros, rejeros, libros de yervas, de animales, aves, de cosmographía, esperas, notomías y una enfinidad, los quales vienen de Francia, Ytalia y Flandes que se ynpriman acá pues es servicio de Dios y bien de la República."

33. I thank Professor Felipe Pereda, an extraordinary connoisseur of artists in sixteenth-century Salamanca, for kindly providing me with this information.

34. Ms. II/2225, Real Biblioteca, Madrid. I discuss this report in "Contrarreforma y tipografía. ¿Nada más que rosarios en sus manos?" *Cuadernos de Historia Moderna* 16 (1995): 73–87.

35. "Alemania, Inglaterra y las demás Provincias que se han inficionado."

36. "Ya no nos quedaba otro remedio contra las blasfemias que aquí pasan, sino el imprimir libros para reprimirlas." "Carta de Francisco Hurtado de Mendoza a Felipe II, Viena, 18 de octubre 1573" ("Letter from Francisco Hurtado de Mendoza to Philip II, Vienna, October 18, 1573"), in *Correspondencia de los príncipes de Alemania con Felipe II y de los embajadores de éste en la corte de Viena (1556 a 1598)*, edited by the Marquis de la Fuensanta del Valle, vol. 5, Colección de Documentos Inéditos para la Historia de España 113 (Madrid, R. Marco y Viñas, 1895).

37. "Los libros entran adonde los sacerdotes no pueden entrar para dar buen consejo y hazen que los hombres enseñados y compungidos busquen ellos mismos lo que han menester."

38. "Para que todos pudiesen saber que aquel género de libros no se auía de vender."

39. "La nueva manera de escreuir que en nuestro tiempo avemos visto y alcançado."

40. "Tanto en un día se imprime y estampa por un solo hombre, quanto a penas en un año muchos podrían escreuir, por causa de lo qual tanta abundancia de libros ha salido y se ha derramado por todo el mundo que ninguna obra que quiera puede faltar a ningún hombre por más pobre que sea."

41. "Yo querría imprimiésemos estas constituciones porque andan diferentes y hay priora que—sin pensar hacer nada—quita y pone cuando las escriben lo que le parece." St. Teresa of Avila, *Epistolario*, edited by Luis Rodríguez Martínez and Teófanes Egido (Madrid: Espiritualidad, 1984), 761.

42. Ms. 12750, Biblioteca Nacional, Madrid.

43. "En la villa de Valladolid a _____ días del mes de _____ de mill y quinientos y _____. Estando los señores inquisidores _____ en su audiencia de la _____ paresció siendo llamado _____ vezino . . ."

44. "La habla sólo sirve al que la oye y está presente"; writing "permanece e siempre habla" and serves "al ausente, presente y por venir, e al sordo e mudo."

45. "Si no hubiese libros que se dispusiesen y guardasen para las edades presentes y futuras, infructuoso fuera el trabajo que se havía de reducir a preceptos de una tradición desnuda."

46. "Casi siempre con el pecho sobre el bufete y con la pluma en los dedos, escriviendo en su vida lo que para leerse ha menester mucho."

47. *Para ventusidades manencónicas* (excerpt from a letter to the Countess of Atalaia from Jorge de Ataíde, accompanying silver bracelets), ms. 51–II–42, no. 74, Biblioteca da Ajuda, Lisbon.

Chapter 3. Natural History of the Written Text: Authors, Copyists, Printers, Booksellers, and Readers

1. "De grande y hermosa letra"; "todos los curiosos que quisieren ser adevinos, en esta casa hallarán quien les enseñe a adevinar en menos de un quarto de hora, por precio de un real de plata, sin ser por arte mágica ni otros medios reprovados por nuestra fe cathólica."

2. "Por aquí passó tal Príncipe, tal Duque, tal Arçobispo."

3. "Palabras y cosas obscenas y lascivas."

4. "Particularmente en el camino del Mar, que guía a la villa del Grau, donde se veían escritas y pintadas grandes indecencias, escriviendo sobre lo borrado en los puestos donde avía capacidad y espacio algunos documentos provechosos."

5. "A qué manera de libros y letras es ynclinado." *Memorial de cláusulas para concertar el matrimonio de Beatriz de Toledo, Marquesa de Jarandilla* (*Account of Clauses for the Arrangement of Marriage to Beatriz de Toledo, Marquise of Jarandilla,* Oropesa, 1589), Frías, Caja 119, Archivo Histórico Nacional-Sección Nobleza, Toledo.

6. "Para poderse dello aprovechar quando fuere menester."

7. Agustín, *Alveolus* (cited in Chapter 1); Gómez de Castro, *Cartapacio manual de notata* (*Handbook of Notes*), ms. k.III.13, Biblioteca de San Lorenzo de El Escorial, El Escorial; Velázquez, *El pan quotidiano* (*Daily Bread*), ms. 73–272, Biblioteca Francisco de Zabálburu, Madrid; Vázquez de Mármol, *Notata quaedam ex libros quos ad vnguem perlegi* (*Some Notes from Books I Have Read with the Greatest Care*), ms. 9226, Biblioteca Nacional, Madrid.

8. "Que con sólo los cartapaçios les basta y se pasan y salen a vezes más bachilleres que los demás."

9. "Començar a escrivir nuevas obras."

10. "Nunca fuy tan feliz que pudiesse escusar a lo menos tres originales de cada uno [y] algunos me cuestan quatro y cinco y aun más."

11. "Una de las mayores [tentaciones] es ponerle [el demonio] a un hombre en el entendimiento que puede componer e imprimir un libro con que gane tanta fama como dineros, y tantos dineros cuanta fama."

12. *Privilege* in English (license and rights to publication); *licencia y privilegio* also designated the letters patent confirming those rights, typically printed at the beginning of books and called in English the *privilege leaf.* Translators' note.

13. The first two terms might be suitably translated as "papers" and "odds and ends"; the last term referred to all manner of single-page texts, such as prayers, litanies, notices, proclamations, and so forth. Translators' note.

14. "Amigo mirón, si me pediste prestado lee, y calla, y quando no alabes el cuidado, encubre algún descuido, como huésped cortés en casa agena. Pero si me compraste, tuyo soy, haz lo que quisieres; sólo te advierto, que no es cordura dizir mal de aquello, porque diste tu dinero. Y te pido que a los mis señores, que juzgan lo que no entienden, y sentencian por las reglas de su gusto, y por las leyes de su passión, des mis besamanos, y vale."

15. "Siempre he pensado que a los libros les suçede lo que a las cassas, que el agrado del esterior, luz y jardines obliga a dessear vivirlos, como a los libros la buena ynpresión a leerlos." Sessa's correspondence is in Lope de Vega Carpio, *Epistolario de Lope de Vega Carpio*, edited by Agustín González de Amezúa (Madrid: Real Academia Española, 1989).

16. "Aunque es verdad que algunas podrá entender un buen juyzio, los libros imprímense para buenos juyzios y para malos." *Memorial a Felipe II sobre las erratas que se dexaron de imprimir en el libro intitulado Imagen de la vida cristiana de fray Héctor Pinto (Report to Philip II Regarding the Errata Printed in the Book Titled "Image of Christian Life" by Friar Heitor Pinto*, Madrid, September 25, 1572), ms. 892, Biblioteca Nacional, Madrid, fol. 192v.

17. "El *Chitón* es verdaderísimo. . . . Leyómele una tarde D. Francisco de Aguilar en un coche en el río. Son çinco pliegos de inpresión, de letra más grande que pequeña, y en las floridas se conoze que es inpreso en Madrid, aunque dize *En Huesca de Aragón*; son las floridas las letras mayores; y este advertimiento me dixo el Padre Nisseno basilio, que tanbien le havía le avía visto, y que el ynpressor era Bernardino de Guzmán." In Lope de Vega Carpio, *Epistolario*.

18. "Hicimos barato de los libros en romance y traducidos de latín, sabiendo ya con ellos los tontos lo que encarecían en otros tiempos los sabios; que ya hasta el lacayo latiniza y hallarán a Horacio en castellano en la caballeriza."

19. The first part of *Don Quixote* is prefaced by a series of mock dedicatory poems, signed by fictional characters. In accordance with the humor of the preliminaries, several are *coplas de cabo roto*, that is, stanzas of seven-syllable verses which all end in words that only rhyme when truncated by one syllable. It was the job of the reader to supply the missing syllable to make complete eight-syllable lines and sense of the words, in this case *judi-cious* and *gulli-ble*, standing in for Cervantes's "bue-[nos]" and "boquirru-[bios]." Translators' note.

20. "Eres tan vario que por poco no te llamo camaleón, animalejo inconstante en la variedad de colores con que se viste."

21. *Justa literaria en loor y alabança del bienaventurado sant Juan Evangelista: Año MDXXXI*. Seville, 1531 or 1532.

22. "Dando el primer lugar al papel que de seys primero saliesse y el segundo al que segundo saliesse y assí todos." *Justa literaria*, introductory material.

23. "El lector que quiere ser buen juez lea primero lo de todos y entonces déles el lugar que a su parescer cada qual meresce y desta manera no terná quexa de los juezes el que no lleva el premio, ni serán los señores juezes juzgados de los que de esta hecha quedarán por juezes y quien quisiere tomar el trabajo leyendo haga vencedor al que quisiere y escribir lo de todos por el orden que quisiere, que está en su mano."

24. "Comienza el sueño. Quien quisiere proseguir la historia, passe a la tercera parte."

25. Early modern and medieval systems of punctuation differ significantly from modern practices. Where we would now place a period marking the end of a sentence, as opposed to a comma, which indicates a parenthetical or subordinate element, scribes and early printers often used the same mark (such as a colon), which served simply to indicate a pause and gave little or no information about the syntax of the passage. Translators' note.

26. "El modo que se ha de tener leyendo esta tragicomedia."

27. "Dizen pío lector, que la leona pare al hijo rudo, y indistincto de miembros, y que después lamiéndolo con la lengua lo va poco a poco figurando, y le dan en cierto modo nueva forma con la lengua. Éste mi libro es parte de mi entendimiento, que oy sale al mundo, y a los ojos de todos rudo, y indistincto, la lengua del benévolo lector haziendo con él el oficio de piedosa madre le ha de dar nueva forma."

28. "Que le sean leydos cuando come, o de noche en el ynvierno después que ha cenado o en otros tiempos, por quien su alteza manda que lea."

29. "Si hera en tiempo de ymbierno leanle chrónicas y gentiles historias," ms. 1869948, Biblioteca Nacional, Madrid. The prince died in 1535.

30. "La Sagrada Escritura y Sanctos Doctores de la Iglesia."

31. "2 tomi di Tacito in penna"; "Coplas de Don Luys de Góngora"; "la Gazzetta di Roma"; "una lettera d'Antonio Perez."

32. "Los haga copiar con cuidado, que el escritor no pierda esas ojas, porque no ay otras en el mundo."

33. "Los tienen todos"; "con . . . condición de que, en trasladándolos, se los bolvería legalmente."

34. "Una carta del Padre Federico . . . y otra en su respuesta del Conde de los Arcos, discreta, prudente y que le castigava asaz de su atrevimiento."

35. "Dexó escribir que el hazer mala letra era de Cavalleros; y no es assí, por ser notorio ay muchos que escriven muy airoso y bien, y se precian dello; y los que no lo hazen les suzede lo que al resto de la República, que por no usarlo se quedaron aun con peor forma que tenían en la escuela."

Chapter 4. Classrooms, Libraries, and Archives as the Culmination of Human Memory

1. "El hombre que no sabe leer, escribir y contar, perfecto hombre no se puede llamar, pues esta habilidad es la más necesaria, y oportuno remedio

para alimentarse y conservarse en cualquier tiempo y comodidad y sin ella no está dispuesto el hombre para ocupación de lucimiento, sino para empleos muy viles y bajos y aun en ésos tiene necesidad de saber escribir, aunque sea muy poco. Y así ninguno o desprecie y aprovéchese cuanto en sí pudiere y estime estos documentos y razones que con todo amor se los propone el Maestro Alonso González Bastones." "Muestra" ("Sample"), in *Maestros españoles. Muestras originales* (*Spanish Masters: Original Samples*). Ms. R.632, Museo Pedagógico, Madrid.

2. "Han exercitado la enseñança de los primeros rudimentos."

3. "Uno se quexa que le maltratan, aquél que le ponen nombres; otro que le quitan la tinta, el delicado que le manchan el papel y borran la plana, quien con los punteros haze pedaços las hojas de los libros y cartillas."

4. "Ponerles nombres [y] componer cantares."

5. "Algunos hombres que se quedaron sin oficio se ponen a ser maestros."

6. "Sumar y restar y multiplicar y medio partir y partir por entero."

7. "Las calidades que a de buscar el varón en la muger con quien se a de casar"; "que busque muger que no sepa escrevir, y aun no la devría desechar porque no supiese leer, porque como la muger no a de tener libro de caxa, ny mayor, ni manual (aunque lo requiera el trato y manera de bivir del marido) ny a de negociar la hazienda, ny arrendar las dehesas, ny cobrar la renta de los juros o tributos, no ay necessidad de que sepa escrevir, pues no a de usar officio de escrivano público, ny tienen tanta sabiduría . . . para que ayan de administar officios públicos."

8. "Reze ella muy devotamente en unas cuentas y si supiese leer, lea en libros de devoción y de buena doctrina, que el escrevir quédese para los hombres. Sepa ella muy bien usar de una aguja, de un huso y una rueca, que no a menester usar de una pluma."

9. "Como su padre no permitiesse que aprendiesse a escriuir, por las letras que hazía en cosas de red y en otras labores con la aguja vino a escrivir de manera que escriue lo que quiere con mucha facilidad."

10. *Arbitrismo* refers to the political and social advice offered by so-called *arbitristas*, promoters of typically utopian schemes for the improvement of the body politic, in this case, "biblioclastic" because they were hostile to books and the promotion of bookish learning. Translators' note.

11. "Reduzir tantas escuelas de escribir y de gramática a menor número, en que a los muchachos (por el interés de sus maestros) se les defrauda y consume el tiempo, que avían de gastar en aprender oficios en beneficio común."

12. "La ocasión de la comunicación alienta a desterrar a tantos de sus propias tierras, con sólo las alas de la pluma y libros, quitándolos de la perseverancia y virtud del trabajo en sus oficios, en que están dependientes unos de otros."

13. The Spanish colleges (*colegios*) were analogous in many ways to the colleges in English universities, with an important difference in that most of them (called *colegios menores*) were founded for undergraduates, rather than

graduates who would take on undergraduate boarders or pupils, as was the case in England. In contrast, the wealthier *colegios mayores,* aimed at producing a scholarly elite, required that their members hold a baccalaureate; admission was competitive, and members enjoyed privileges such as full financial support so that they could prepare advanced degrees. During the period covered by this study, there were six *colegios mayores.* Translators' note.

14. "No alcanzo a comprender todavía por qué mal hado los hombres graves de Salamanca y los primeros en sus escuelas, de seguida aspiran a la administración de la república y a sus honores—para gobernar a su arbitrio todas las cosas—con tanto menosprecio de la elocuencia." I quote according to Alonso García de Matamoros, *Pro adserenda hispanorum eruditione,* edited and translated by José López de Toro, *Revista de Filología Española* Anejo 28 (Madrid: Aldecoa, 1943), 211.

15. "La suma de la civilidad"; "en ir pulcramente vestidos y en no hablar latín por lo difícil que resulta."

16. "Escuchaban a los filósofos, leían sus libros y meditaban sus preceptos. ¡Bello espectáculo el de los príncipes guerreros que defendían causas en el foro y disputaban con los filósofos en las escuelas!"

17. "No le es necesario ni de provecho." *Memoriales diferentes de la cassa de S. M. y altezas Príncipes de Ungría y otras cosas* (*Different Reports from the House of His Majesty and their Royal Highnesses the Princes of Hungary and Other Matters*), ms. 26 V 20 (formerly Envío 134), Instituto Valencia de Don Juan, Madrid.

18. "O Philipinho Príncipe nunca quis aprender latim." *Miscellânea de curiosidades históricas* (*Miscellany of Historical Curiosities*), Cod. 560, Biblioteca Nacional, Lisbon, fol.10v.

19. "In sondables océanos"; "nadar . . . con mi corta barquilla." "Carta del muy noble y erudito portugués Manuel de Faria e Sousa" ("Letter from the very noble and erudite Portuguese Manuel de Faria y Sousa"), in Gerónimo Fuser, *Vida del venerable y apostólico varón . . . Fray Gerónimo Batista de Lanuza* (*Life of the Venerable and Apostolic Man . . . Friar Gerónimo Batista de Lanuza,* Zaragoza, 1648).

20. "Que no me ando a buscar las librerías / de arzobispos ni duques ni marqueses / que las tienen por sus fanfarronías / y leen en los libros pocas veces." Quixada's *Response* appears at the beginning of the manuscript edited by Gayangos: Bartolomé de Villalba y Estañá, *El peregrino curioso y grandezas de España,* ed. Pascual de Gayangos (Madrid: M. Ginesta, 1886–89), 68.

21. "El modo cómo se debría haber un ombre de mi calidad si llegase a la graçia de su Príncipe"; "la razón con que se pueda governar un señor en sus estados"; "tan separados y algunos tan çeñidos de otros dueños poderosos que pienso que sería llebar en las manos el sol para ver y discernir tan escuras dificultades."

22. "No piensan que le tocan al dueño de los lugares más de los frutos."

23. "Se halla el camino de la plática con más fácil y segura inteligencia."

24. "Muertos son, y que ningún accidente puede resuçitarlos."

25. "Sus materias tocan por ventura a los que no estamos lexos de gouier-nos, y yo estoy codicioso de rebolverlos, pues no daña este género de manus-critos a los que vamos haçiendo actos."

26. "Muchos libros y papeles que andaban esparcidos en diferentes partes . . . [que] los más dellos son tocantes a materias graves y de importancia que se trataron en tiempo del Emperador Carlos quinto, mi bisabuelo, y de los reyes mis señores, abuelo y padre que santa gloria hayan, que algunos dellos son originales." This subject is treated in my article, "Guardar papeles—y quemarlos—en tiempos de Felipe II: La documentación de Juan de Zúñiga (Un capítulo para la historia del Fondo Altamira)," Part 1, *Reales Sitios* 33 (1996): 2–15; and Part 2, 34 (1997): 19–33.

27. "Otras naciones"; "para memoria de la posteridad."

28. "Aquel indio era el archivista o, por dezir mexor, el archivo de aquel pueblo."

29. "Fiestas que se hizieron en la imperial ciudad de Toledo por la conver-sión del Reyno de Inglaterra."

30. "La letra siguiente en unos papelitos escrita": "Aquí la brava ser-piente / de humana carnalidad / baxe el cuello a la verdad / tire el carro humildemente."

31. Ms. 9175, Biblioteca Nacional, Madrid.

32. "Celestinas con su cuchillada y sus canasticas de olores." The passage refers to the eponymous main character of the European bestseller attributed to Fernando de Rojas, most widely known as *Celestina* but published originally as the *Comedia* (and later *Tragicomedia*) *de Calisto y Melibea* (1499); Celestina is an old bawd who serves as go-between for the two protagonists, while running her brothel now in decline and selling makeup and perfume to local women, among other trades. She sports a scar from a knife wound on her face. Trans-lators' note.

Bibliography

Primary Sources—Manuscripts

Algunos hechos famosos y genealogía de la Casa de los Gonzaga. Ms. M 5, Biblioteca Universitaria, Valencia.

Ataide, Jorge de. "Para ventusidades manencónicas." Excerpt from a letter to the Countess of Atalaia from Jorge de Ataíde, accompanying the gift of some silver bracelets. Ms. 51-II-42, n° 74, Biblioteca da Ajuda, Lisbon.

Carta de Vespasiano Gonzaga a Mateo Vázquez de Lecca remitiendo el dibujo de una persona monstruosa, Valencia, 21 de octubre de 1571(?). Instituto Valencia de Don Juan, Madrid.

Cavide, Álvaro. *Arte para conocernos a nosotros mismos por señales exteriores.* Ms. 2843, Biblioteca Nacional, Madrid.

Creswell, Joseph. *Memorial para la provisión de libros católicos.* Ms. II/2225, Real Biblioteca, Madrid.

Discurso de la comparación de la antigua y moderna pintura y escultura. Ms. 19639, Biblioteca Nacional, Madrid.

Doctrina del Príncipe de Piamonte. Ms.1869948, Biblioteca Nacional, Madrid.

Fernández de Velasco, Juan. *Relación enviada a Felipe II sobre las jurisdicciones de Milán y conflictos con el Arzobispo Borromeo* (Milán, c. 1595). Ms. 12851, Biblioteca Nacional, Madrid.

Gómez de Castro, Alvar. *Cartapacio manual de notata.* Ms. k.III.13, Biblioteca de San Lorenzo de El Escorial, El Escorial.

González Bastones, Alonso. "Muestra." *Maestros españoles. Muestras originales.* Ms. R.632, Museo Pedagógico, Madrid.

Memorial de cláusulas para concertar el matrimonio de Beatriz de Toledo, Marquesa de Jarandilla (Oropesa, 1589). Ms. Frías, Caja 119, Archivo Histórico Nacional-Sección Nobleza, Toledo.

Memorial de la rreductión de Inglaterra al gremio o unión de la sancta madre Iglesia. Ms. 9175, Biblioteca Nacional, Madrid.

Memoriales diferentes de la cassa de S. M. y altezas Príncipes de Ungría y otras cosas. Ms. 26 V 20 (formerly Envío 134), Instituto Valencia de Don Juan, Madrid.

Miscellânea de curiosidades históricas. Cod. 560, Biblioteca Nacional, Lisbon.

Olivares, Adiosdado de. *Memoriales y cartas presentadas al concilio provincial de Salamanca* (1566). Casa de Cadaval, maço 17, Arquivo Nacional da Torre do Tombo, Lisbon.

Orellana, Joan de. *Juiçio de las leyes civiles.* Ms. 17787, Biblioteca Nacional, Madrid.

Portocarrero, Pedro. *Carta familiar del Obispo de Calahorra, Pedro Portocarrero, sobre las misiones de interior* (Logroño, 1593). Patronato Eclesiástico, 40, Archivo General, Simancas.

Rolim de Moura, Francisco. *Instruçiones de reglas de Juan de Vega con el comento de Dom Francisco Rolim senhor de las vilhas de Azambuja, Monteargil y Marmelar.* Ms. 51-II-42, no. 41, Biblioteca da Ajuda, Lisbon.

Soares, Diogo. *Memorial sobre las razones por las que no se debe imprimir la Historia que trata de la guerra de Pernambuco por Duarte de Albuquerque* (c. 1644). Ms. Add. 28401, British Library, London.

Torre, Diego de la. *Memorial figurado enviado por Diego de la Torre a Felipe II* (Tunja, 1584). Mapas, Planos y Dibujos XXVI–60, Archivo General, Simancas.

Vázquez de Mármol, Juan. *Notata quaedam ex libros quos ad vnguem perlegi.* Ms. 9226, Biblioteca Nacional, Madrid.

———. *Memorial a Felipe II sobre las erratas que se dexaron de imprimir en el libro intitulado Imagen de la vida cristiana de fray Héctor Pinto* (Madrid, 1572). Ms. 892, Biblioteca Nacional, Madrid.

Velázquez, Pedro. *El pan quotidiano.* Ms. 73-272. Biblioteca Francisco de Zabálburu, Madrid.

Printed Works Before 1700

Angulo, Juan de. *Flor de solemnes alegrías.* Toledo, 1555.

Belvis Trejo, Alonso de. *Forma breve que se ha de tener en soltar o correr la mano en el exercicio de escribir liberal. Y para que las personas que no hazen buena letra la mejoren.* Toledo, 1678.

Cardona, Juan Bautista. *De expugnendis haereticorum propriis nominibus etiam de libris que de religione ex profeso non tractant.* Rome, 1576.

Ceballos, Blas Antonio de. *Libro histórico y moral sobre el origen y excelencias del nobilíssimo arte de leer, escribir y contar y su enseñanza. Perfecta instrucción para educar a la jubentud en virtud y letras. Santos y maestros insignes que han exercitado la enseñança de los primeros rudimentos.* Madrid, 1692.

Cervera de la Torre, Antonio. *Testimonio auténtico y verdadero de las cosas notables que pasaron en la . . . muerte de . . . Phelipe II.* Valencia, 1599.

Coplas que acostumbran cantar en sus missiones los padres missionistas del convento de Nuestra Señora del Pilar de las montañas de Jaca. (n.p., n.d.)

Díaz Morante, Pedro. *Segunda parte del arte de escribir.* Madrid, 1624.

Enríquez de Zúñiga, Juan. *Amor con vista. Lleva una sumaria descripción del mundo, ansí de la parte elemental come de la aethérea.* Cuenca, 1634.

Faria e Sousa, Manuel de. *El gran justicia de Aragón.* Madrid, 1650.

Francis de Sales, St. *Vida simbólica del glorioso S. Francisco de Sales . . . dividida en dos partes y escrita en cinqüenta y dos emblemas.* Translated by Bartolomé de Alcázar. Madrid, 1688.

Fresneda, Francisco de. "Sermón que predicó el muy R. P. Fray Francisco de Fresneda, lector jubilado y guardián de san Francisco de la Ciudad de Vélez Málaga." *Libro de todos los sermones que se predicaron en diferentes ciudades, en las horras y cabo de año del Illustríssimo y Reverendíssimo señor Don Juan Alonso de Moscoso, Obispo que fue de las Sanctas Yglesias de Guadix y León, y Málaga, electo Arçobispo de Santiago, del Consejo de su Magestad. Passó desta vida a la eterna a 21 de agosto de 1614 años.* Málaga, 1617(?).

Fuser, Gerónimo. *Vida del venerable y apostólico varón, el illmo. y Rmo. S. don Fray Gerónimo Batista de Lanuza de la Orden de los predicadores, obispo de Barbastro.* Saragossa: 1648.

García, Marcos. *La flema de Pedro Hernández: Discurso moral y político añadido y enmendado por su autor.* Madrid, 1657.

Hinojosa y Carvajal, Álvaro de. *Libro de la vida y milagros de S. Inés con otras varias rimas a lo divino.* Braga, 1611.

Jáuregui, Juan de. *Memorial informatorio por los pintores.* Published in *Diálogos de la pintura: su defensa, origen, essencia, definición, modos y diferencias, al gran monarcha de las Españas y Nuevo Mundo, don Felipe IIII,* by Vicente Carducho. Madrid: Francisco Martínez, 1633.

Juan de Santa María. *Dichoso fin a la vida humana y feliz tránsito a la eterna de el gran monarca Felipe Quarto Rey de las Españas . . . Dispuesta su reimpressión por Maestre de Campo D. Diego Xarava del Castillo . . . Castellano del Obispo de dicha Ciudad.* Madrid, 1667; Naples: 1675.

Justa literaria en loor y alabança del bienaventurado sant Juan Evangelista. Año MDXXXI. Seville, 1531 or 1532.

Maldonado y Pardo, José. *Museo o biblioteca selecta del excelentísimo señor don Pedro Núñez de Guzmán, Marqués de Montealegre.* Madrid, 1677.

Naja, Martín de la. *El missionero perfecto.* Saragossa, 1678.

Navarra Labrit, Pedro de. *Diálogos de la differencia del hablar al escrevir.* Tolosa, 1565.

Ovalle, Alonso de. *Histórica relación del Reyno de Chile, de las missiones y ministerios que exercita en él la Compañía de Jesús.* Rome, 1646.

Palafox y Mendoza, Juan de. *Bocados espirituales, políticos, místicos y morales. Catecismo y axiomas doctrinales para labradores y gente sencilla.* Madrid, 1667.

Pascual, Miguel Ángel. *El oyente preservado y fortalecido en una missión practicada.* Valencia, 1698.

Por el agricoltura, criança, artífizes, marinería del Reyno. Contra el exceso de libros nuevos y mal uso en las ciencias, física, medicina, jurisprudencia, matemática, astrología y otros abusos y costumbres en las profesiones de las repúblicas democrática, aristocrática y monarquía y su mejor gobierno. De el príncipe sucessivo y electivo. Su poder temporal y obligación de su cargo en justicia, en paz y en guerra y de la obediencia que deven el vassallo, súbdito y esempto y oficios públicos. Seville(?), 1633.

Relación de lo que el rey nuestro señor ha resuelto para el bien, conservación y seguridad destos Reynos, alivio y descanso de sus vassallos con acuerdo de la junta que ha mandado hazer de los Presidentes y algunos de su Consejo y otros ministros y personas de diferentes tribunales y professiones y de la Diputación del Reyno a que ha asistido su real persona. Madrid, 1622.

Rojas Villandrando, Agustín de. *El buen repúblico.* Salamanca, 1611.

Román, Jerónimo. *Segunda parte de las repúblicas del mundo.* Salamanca, 1595.

Salinas, Miguel de. *Rethórica en lengua castellana en la qual se pone muy en breve lo necessario para saber bien hablar y escrevir y conoscer quién habla y escrive bien.* Alcalá de Henares, 1541.

Sánchez, Pedro. *Árbol de consideración y varia doctrina plantado en el campo fertilíssimo de los memorables mysterios de la Semana Sancta. Del qual se cortan ramos muy hermosos que se reparten a los que van en la processión el Domingo de Ramos, uno para cada día desta semana. Y son siete consideraciones principales de la Passión del Redemptor. Y estos ramos están cargados de flores y frutos de otras materias agradables y provechosas para todo christiano en qualquier tiempo. Una adición de los mysterios de la Resurrectión del Redemptor, y la vida de Adam y la del Antichristo y la de los siete durmientes y otras cosas dignas de saber.* Toledo, 1584.

Soares, Vicente Gusmão. *Rimas varias en alabança del nacimiento del Príncipe N. S. Don Balthazar Carlos Domingo.* Oporto, 1630.

Thámara, Francisco de. *Livro de Polidoro Vergilio que tracta de la invención y principio de todas las cosas. Agora nuevamente traduzido y trasladado en lengua castellana para doctrina y exemplo.* Antwerp, 1550.

Ucedo, Sebastián de. *El príncipe deliberante abstracto en idioma castellano.* Cologne, 1678.

Vega, Pedro de. *Segunda parte de la declaración de los siete salmos penitenciales.* Madrid, 1602.

Vera y Zúñiga, Juan de. *El Fernando o Sevilla Restaurada. Poema heroico escrito con los versos de la Gerusalemme Liberata de Torquato Tasso.* Milan, 1632.

Vieira, António. "Sermón del Viernes Sexto de Quaresma. Predicado en la Capilla Real. Año de 1662." In Vieira, *Sermones.* Barcelona, 1685.

Vilhegas, Diogo Henriques de. *Leer sin libro. Direcciones acertadas para el govierno éthico, económico y político.* Lisbon, 1672.

Modern Editions of Works Before 1700

Agustín, Antonio. *Alveolus: Manuscrito escurialense S–II–18.* Edited and translated by Cándido Flores Sellés. Clásicos Olvidados 6. Madrid: Fundación Universitaria Española, 1982.

Cervantes Saavedra, Miguel de. *Don Quijote de la Mancha.* Edited by Francisco Rico and Joaquín Forradellas. Barcelona: Crítica, 2001.

Correas, Gonzalo de. *Vocabulario de refranes y frases proverbiales.* Edited by Víctor Infantes. Biblioteca Filológica Hispana 8. Madrid: Visor, 1992.

Correspondencia de los príncipes de Alemania con Felipe II y de los embajadores de éste en la corte de Viena (1556 a 1598). Edited by the Marquis of La Fuensanta del Valle. Vol. 5. Colección de Documentos Inéditos para la Historia de España 113. Madrid: R. Marco y Viñas, 1895.

Da Sommaia, Girolamo. *Diario de un estudiante de Salamanca: Crónica inédita de Girolamo da Sommaia*. Edited by George Haley. Acta Salmanticensia: Historia de la Universidad 27. Salamanca: Universidad de Salamanca, Secretariado de Publicaciones e Intercambio Científico, 1977.

García de Matamoros, Alonso. *Pro adserenda hispanorum eruditione*. Edited and translated by José López de Toro. Madrid: Aldecoa, 1943.

Macedo, António de Sousa. *Eva y Ave o Maria triunfante*. Translated by Diego Suárez de Figueroa. Madrid, 1631. Murcia: M. Tornel y Olmos, 1882.

Machado, Félix, Marqués de Montebelo, *Tercera parte del Guzmán de Alfarache*. Edited by Gerhard Moldenhaner. *Revue Hispanique* 69 (1927): 1–340.

Pecorelli, Alberto. *Il Rè Catholico*. Edited by Juan Beneyto Pérez. Publicaciones del Seminario de Historia de las Doctrinas Politicas 1. Madrid: Consejo Superior de Investigaciones Científicas, Instituto Francisco de Vitoria, 1942.

Quevedo, Francisco de. *Dreams and Discourses/ Sueños y discursos*. Edited and translated by R. K. Britton. Hispanic Classics. Warminster, UK: Aris and Phillips, 1989.

Teresa of Avila, Saint. *Epistolario*. Edited by Luis Rodríguez Martínez and Teófanes Egido. Madrid: Espiritualidad, 1984.

Vega Carpio, Lope de. *Epistolario de Lope de Vega Carpio*. Edited by Agustín González de Amezúa. Madrid: Real Academia Española, 1989. 4 vols.

———. *Fuente Ovejuna*. Edited and translated by Victor Dixon. Hispanic Classics. Warminster, UK: Aris and Phillips, 1989.

The Life of Lazarillo de Tormes/ La vida de Lazarillo de Tormes y de sus fortunas y adversidades. Translated by David Rowland (1653) and edited by Keith Whitlock. Hispanic Classics. Warminster, UK: Aris and Phillips, 2000.

Villalba y Estañá, Bartolomé de. *El pelegrino curioso y grandezas de España*. Edited by Pascual de Gayangos. Madrid: M. Ginesta, 1886–89.

Zabaleta, Juan de. *Errores celebrados*. Edited by David Hershberg. Madrid: Espasa-Calpe, 1972.

Secondary Sources

Álvarez Santaló, León Carlos. "El libro de devoción como modelo y modelador de la conducta social: el 'Luz a los vivos' de Palafox." *Trocadero* 1 (1989): 7–25.

Amelang, James. *The Flight of Icarus: Artisan Autobiography in Early Modern Europe*. Stanford, Calif.: Stanford University Press, 1998.

Antón Pelayo, Javier. *La herencia cultural: Alfabetización y lectura en la ciudad de Gerona (1747–1807)*. Bellaterra: Universidad Autónoma de Barcelona, 1998.

Antonucci, Laura. "La escrittura giudicata: Perizie grafiche in processi romani del primo Seicento." *Scritura e civiltà* 13 (1989): 489–534.

Asensio, Eugenio. "Censura inquisitorial de libros en los siglos XVI y XVII. Fluctuaciones. Decadencia." In *El libro antiguo español: Actas del primer coloquio internacional (Madrid, 18 al 20 de diciembre de 1986)* Salamanca: Universidad de Salamanca, 1988. 21–36.

Baker, Edward. *La biblioteca de Don Quijote.* Madrid: Marcial Pons, 1997.

Baranda, Nieves. "Escritos para la educación de nobles en los siglos XVI y XVII." *La culture des élites espagnoles à l'epoque moderne. Bulletin Hispanique* 97 (1995) : 157–71.

Bataillon, Marcel. "Santa Teresa, lectora de libros de caballerías." In Bataillon, *Varia lección de clásicos españoles.* Translated by José Pérez Riesco. Madrid: Gredos, 1964. 21–23. Collected articles from 1935–1960 translated from the French.

Berger, Philippe. *Libro y lectura en la Valencia del Renacimiento.* Translated by Amparo Balanzá Pérez. Estudios Universitarios 19–20. Valencia: Alfons el Magnànim, 1987. 2 vols. Translation of dissertation, "Livre et lecture à Valence à l'époque de la Renaissance," Université de Bordeaux 3, 1983.

Bernat Vistarini, Antonio and John T. Cull. *Enciclopedia de emblemas españoles ilustrados.* Madrid: Akal, 1999.

Bertière, Simone. "La guerre en images: gravures satiriques anti-espagnoles." In *L'âge d'or de l'influence espagnole: La France et l'Espagne à l'epoque d'Anne d'Autriche, 1615–1666. Actes du 20e Colloque du C.M.R. 17, Bordeaux, 25–28 janvier 1990.* Edited by Charles Mazouer. Mont de Marsan: Interuniversitaires, 1991. 147–83.

Bethencourt, Francisco. *O imaginário da magia: feiticeiras, saludadores e nigromantes no século XVI.* Colecção Temas de Cultura Portuguesa 11. Lisbon: Centro de Estudos de História e Cultura Portuguesa, Projecto Universidade Aberta, 1987.

Blair, Ann. "Humanist Methods and Natural Philosophy: The Commonplace Book." *Journal of the History of Ideas* 53 (1992): 541–51.

Bouza, Fernando. "Cinco piezas para una práctica nobiliaria de la corte." In Bouza, *Capítulos de historia cultural del reinado de Felipe II.* Madrid: Akal, 1998.

———. "Contrarreforma y tipografía. ¿Nada más que rosarios en sus manos?" *Cuadernos de Historia Moderna* 16 (1995): 73–87.

———. *Corre manuscrito: Una historia cultural del Siglo de Oro.* Madrid: Marcial Pons, 2001.

———. "Corte es decepción: Don Juan de Silva, conde de Portalegre." In *La corte de Felipe II.* Edited by José Martínez Millán. Alianza Universidad 798. Madrid: Alianza, 1994. 451–502.

———. *Del escribano a la biblioteca: La civilización escrita europea en la alta Edad Moderna (siglos XV–XVII).* Historia Universal. Historia Moderna, 5. Madrid: Síntesis, 1992.

————. "Docto y devoto: La biblioteca del Marqués de Almazán y Conde de Monteagudo (Madrid, 1591)." In *Hispania-Austria II: Die Epoche Philipps II (1556–1598)*. Edited by Friedrich Edelmayer. Studien zur Geschichte und Kultur der iberischen und iberoamerikanischen Länder 5. Munich: R. Oldenbourg, 1999. 247–310.

————. "Guardar papeles—y quemarlos—en tiempos de Felipe II. La documentación de Juan de Zúñiga (Un capítulo para la historia del Fondo Altamira)." Part 1. *Reales Sitios* 33 (1996): 2–15; Part 2 34 (1997): 19–33.

————. *Imagen y propaganda: Capítulos de historia cultural del reinado de Felipe II*. Akal Universitaria. Serie Historia Moderna 200. Madrid: Akal, 1998.

————. *Locos, enanos y hombres de placer en la corte de los Austrias*. Madrid: Temas de Hoy, 1991, 1996.

————. "La majestad de Felipe II. Construcción del mito real." *La corte de Felipe II*. Edited by José Martínez Millán. Alianza Universidad 798. Madrid: Alianza, 1994. 37–72.

————. *Palabra e imagen en la Corte: Cultura oral y visual de la nobleza en al Siglo de Oro*. Madrid: Abada Editores, 2003.

————. "¿Para qué imprimir? de autores, público, impresores y manuscritos en el Siglo de Oro." *Cuadernos de Historia Moderna* (Madrid) 18 (1997): 31–50.

————. *Portugal no tempo dos Felipes: Política, cultura, representações (1580–1668)*. Lisbon: Cosmos, 2000.

Brown, Jonathan. *Kings and Connoisseurs: Collecting Art in Seventeenth-Century Europe*. Princeton, N.J.: Princeton University Press, 1995.

Burke, Peter. *Popular Culture in Early Modern Europe*. New York: New York University Press, 1978.

Cardim, Pedro A. "Entre textos y discursos. La historiografía y el poder del lenguaje." *Cuadernos de Historia Moderna* 17 (1996): 123–49.

Carruthers, Mary. *The Book of Memory: A Study of Memory in Medieval Culture*. Cambridge: Cambridge University Press, 1990.

Casares, Emilio. "Espina, Juan de." *Biografías y documentos sobre música y músicos españoles*. By Francisco Asenjo Barbieri, edited by Casares. Legado Barbieri 1. Madrid: Fundación Banco Exterior, 1986.

Castillo Gómez, Antonio. "'Amanecieron en todas las partes públicas . . .': Un viaje al país de las denuncias." In *Escribir y leer en el siglo de Cervantes*, ed. Antonio Castillo Gómez. Barcelona: Gedisa, 1999. 143–91.

————. "Del signo negado al signo virtual. Cambios y permanencias en la historia social de la cultura escrita." *Signo* 6 (1999): 113–43.

————. "Entre publique et privé: Stratégies de l'écrit dans l'Espagne du Siècle d'Or." *Annales: Histoire, Sciences Sociales* 56 (2001): 803–29.

————. *Escrituras y escribientes: Prácticas de la cultura escrita en una ciudad del Renacimiento*. Las Palmas: Fundación de Enseñanza Superior a Distancia de Las Palmas de Gran Canaria, 1997.

Cátedra, Pedro M., ed. *La* Doctrina cristiana del ermitaño y niño *de Andrés Flórez, O.P. (Valladolid, 1552)*. Salamanca: (n.p.), 1997.

———. *Invención, difusión y recepción de la literatura popular impresa (siglo XVI)*. Mérida: Editora Regional de Extremadura, 2002.

Cátedra, Pedro M. and María Luisa López-Vidriero. *La imprenta y su impacto en Castilla*. Salamanca: (n.p.), 1998.

Cavallo, Guglielmo. "I libri del decoro." In *I luoghi della memoria scritta: Manoscriti, incunabili, libri a stampa di biblioteche statali italiane*. Edited by Guglielmo Cavallo. Rome: Istituto Poligrafico e Zecca dello Stato, Libreria dello Stato, 1994. 103–240.

Cavallo, Guglielmo and Roger Chartier, eds. A *History of Reading in the West*. Oxford: Polity Press, 1999.

Cayuela, Anne. *Le paratexte au Siècle d'Or: Prose romanesque, livres et lecteurs en Espagne au XVIIe siècle*. Travaux du Grand Siècle 5. Geneva: Droz, 1996.

Certeau, Michel de. *The Practice of Everyday Life*. Translated by Steven Rendall. Berkeley: University of California Press, 1984.

Chartier, Roger. *The Cultural Uses of Print in Early Modern France*. Translated by Lydia G. Cochrane. Princeton, N.J.: Princeton University Press, 1987.

———. "Culture écrite et littérature à l'âge moderne." *Annales: Histoire, Sciences Sociales* 56 (July–September 2001): 783–802.

———. *Culture écrite et société: L'ordre des livres (XIVe–XVIIIe siècles)*. Paris: Albin Michel, 1996.

———. "Del libro a la lectura: Lectores populares en el Renacimiento." *Bulletin Hispanique* 99 (1997): 309–24.

———. *On the Edge of the Cliff: History, Language, and Practices*. Translated by Lydia G. Cochrane. Baltimore: Johns Hopkins University Press, 1995.

———. *The Order of Books: Readers, Authors, and Libraries in Europe Between the Fourteenth and Eighteenth Centuries*. Translated by Lydia G. Cochrane. Stanford, Calif.: Stanford University Press, 1994.

Chartier, Roger and Hans-Jürgen Lüsebrink, eds. *Colportage et lecture populaire: Imprimés de large circulation en Europe, XVIe–XIXe siècle*. Paris: IMEC Editions et Editions de la Maison de Sciences de l'Homme, 1996.

Chevalier, Maxime. *Lectura y lectores en la España de los siglos XVI y XVII*. Madrid: Turner, 1976.

Cruickshank, D. W. "Literature and the Book Trade in Golden Age Spain." *Modern Language Review* 73 (1978): 799–824.

Dadson, Trevor J. *Libros, lecturas y lectores: Estudios sobre bibliotecas particulares españolas del Siglo de Oro*. Instrumenta Bibliológica. Madrid: Arco Libros, 1998.

Davis, Natalie Zemon. *Society and Culture in Early Modern France*. Stanford, Calif.: Stanford University Press, 1975.

Delgado, Juan. "Bibliografía sobre justas poéticas." *Edad de Oro* 7 (1988): 197–207.

Egido, Aurora. "Los manuales de escribientes desde el Siglo de Oro: Apuntes para la teoría de la escritura." *Bulletin Hispanique* 97 (1995): 67–94.

Eisenstein, Elizabeth. *The Printing Press as an Agent of Change: Communications and Cultural Transformations in Early Modern Europe.* 2 vols. Cambridge: Cambridge University Press, 1979.

———. *The Printing Revolution in Early Modern Europe.* Cambridge: Cambridge University Press, 1994.

Evangelisti, Claudia. "'Libelli famosi': Processi per scritte infamanti nella Bologna di fine '500." *Annali della Fondazione Einaudi* 27 (1992): 181–239.

Ferreira, Carlos A. "D. Francisco de Portugal: Elementos para su bio-bibliografía." *Biblos* 22 (1946): 607–73.

Fleming, Juliet. *Graffiti and the Writing Arts of Early Modern England.* Philadelphia: University of Pennsylvania Press, 2001.

Flor, Fernando Rodríguez de la. *Biblioclasmo: Por una práctica crítica de la lecto-escritura.* Valladolid: Junta de Castilla y León, Consejería de Educación y Cultura, 1997.

———. *La península metafísica: Arte, literatura y pensamiento en la España de la Contrarreforma.* Colección Metrópoli 7. Madrid: Biblioteca Nueva, 1999.

Foucault, Michel. *The Order of Things: An Archeology of the Human Sciences.* New York: Pantheon, 1970.

Fox, Adam. "Ballads, Libels and Popular Ridicule in Jacobean England." *Past and Present* 145 (1994): 47–83.

———. *Oral and Literate Culture in England, 1500–1700.* Oxford: Clarendon Press, 2000.

Freedberg, David. *The Power of Images: Studies in the History and Theory of Response.* Chicago: University of Chicago Press, 1989.

Frenk Alatorre, Margit. *Entre la voz y el silencio.* Biblioteca de Estudios Cervantinos 4. Alcalá de Henares: Centro de Estudios Cervantinos, 1977.

———. "Lectores y oidores: La difusión oral de la literatura en el Siglo de Oro." In *Actas del VII Congreso de la Asociación Internacional de Hispanistas.* Vol. 1. Rome: Bulzoni, 1982. 101–23.

Gacto Fernández, E. "Inquisición y censura en el Barroco." In *Sexo barroco y otras transgresiones premodernas.* Edited by Francisco Tomás y Valiente. Alianza Universidad 662. Madrid: Alianza, 1990. 153–72.

Gállego, Julián. *El pintor, de artesano a artista.* Granada: Universidad de Granada, Departamento de Historia del Arte, 1976.

———. *Vision et symboles dans la peinture espagnole du siècle d'or.* Collection Le Signe de l'Art 3. Paris: Klincksieck, 1968.

Gan Giménez, Pedro. "La jornada de Felipe III a Portugal (1619)." *Chronica Nova* 19 (1991): 407–31.

García Cárcel, Ricardo. *Las culturas del Siglo de Oro.* Biblioteca Historia 16, 3. Madrid: Historia 16, 1989.

García de Enterría, María Cruz. "Lecturas y rasgos de un público." *Edad de Oro* 12 (1993): 119–30.

———. *Sociedad y poesía de cordel en el Barroco.* Persiles 67. Madrid: Taurus, 1973.

García Oro, José. *Los reyes y los libros: La política libraria de la Corona en el Siglo de Oro (1475–1598).* Madrid: Cisneros, 1995.

Gimeno Blay, Francisco. "Analfabetismo y alfabetización femeninos en la Valencia del Quinientos." *Estudis* 19 (1993): 59–101.

Ginzburg, Carlo. *The Cheese and the Worms: The Cosmos of a Sixteenth-Century Miller.* Baltimore: Johns Hopkins University Press, 1980.

González de Amezúa, Agustín. *Cómo se hacía un libro en nuestro Siglo de Oro.* Madrid: Magisterio Español, 1946.

González Sánchez, Carlos Alberto. *Los mundos del libro: Medios de difusión de la cultura occidental en las Indias de los siglos XVI y XVII.* Seville: Universidad de Sevilla, 1999.

Goody, Jack, ed. *Literacy in Traditional Societies.* Cambridge: Cambridge University Press, 1968.

Goyet, Francis. *Le sublime du "lieu commun": L'invention rhétorique à la Renaissance.* Paris: Honoré Champion, 1996.

Grafton, Anthony. *Commerce with the Classics: Ancient Books and Renaissance Readers.* Ann Arbor: University of Michigan Press, 1997.

Griffin, Clive. *The Crombergers of Seville: The History of a Printing and Merchant Dynasty.* Oxford: Clarendon Press, 1988.

Grignon, Claude and Jean-Claude Passeron. *Le savant et le populaire: Misérabilisme et populisme en sociologie et en littérature.* Paris: Gallimard/Seuil, 1989.

Haskell, Francis. *History and Its Images: Art and the Interpretation of the Past.* New Haven, Conn.: Yale University Press, 1993.

Hernández González, Isabel. "Suma de inventarios de bibliotecas del siglo XVI (1501–1560)." In *El libro antiguo español IV: Coleccionismo y bibliotecas (siglos XV–XVII).* Edited by María Luisa López-Vidriero, Pedro M. Cátedra, and María Isabel Hernández González. Salamanca: Universidad de Salamanca, 1998. 375–446.

Herpoel, S. "El lector femenino en el Siglo de Oro español." In *La mujer en la literatura hispánica de la Edad Media y el Siglo de Oro.* Edited by Rina Walthaus. Amsterdam: Rodopi, 1993. 91–99.

Ife, Barry W. *Reading and Fiction in Golden Age Spain.* Cambridge: Cambridge University Press, 1985.

Infantes, Víctor. "De la cartilla al libro." *Bulletin Hispanique* 97 (1995): 33–66.

———. *De las primeras letras: Cartillas y doctrinas españolas de los siglos XV y XVI.* Salamanca: Ediciones Universidad de Salamanca, 1998.

———. "Los pliegos sueltos poéticos: Constitución tipográfica y contenido literario (1482–1600)." In Infantes, *En el Siglo de Oro: Estudios y textos de literatura áurea.* Potomac, Md.: Scripta Humanistica, 1992. 47–52.

Jarauta, Francisco. "Barroco y modernidad." In *Figuras e imágenes del Barroco: Estudios sobre el Barroco español y sobre la obra de Alonso Cano.* Edited by Delfín Rodríguez Ruiz. Debates sobre Arte 9. Madrid: Visor, 1999. 45–48.

Jardine, Lisa and Anthony Grafton. "'Studied for Action': How Gabriel Harvey Read His Livy." *Past and Present* 129 (1990): 30–78.

Jones, Ann Rosalind and Peter Stallybrass. *Renaissance Clothing and the Materials of Memory.* Cambridge: Cambridge University Press, 2000.

Kagan, Richard. *Students and Society in Early Modern Spain.* Baltimore: John Hopkins University, 1974.

Lopez, François. "Libros y papeles." *Bulletin Hispanique* 99 (1997): 293–307.

Love, Harold. *Scribal Publication in Seventeenth-Century England.* Oxford: Clarendon Press, 1993. Reissued as *The Culture and Commerce of Texts: Scribal Publication in Seventeenth-Century England.* Amherst, Mass.: University of Massachusetts Press, 1998.

Marin, Louis. *Des pouvoirs de l'image: Gloses.* Paris: Seuil, 1993.

———. "Lire un tableau: Une lettre de Poussin en 1639." In *Pratiques de la lecture.* Edited by Roger Chartier. Marseille: Rivages, 1985. 102–24.

Marotti, Arthur F. *Manuscript, Print, and the English Renaissance Lyric.* Ithaca, N.Y.: Cornell University Press, 1995.

McKenzie, D. F. *Bibliography and the Sociology of Texts.* The Panizzi Lectures 1985. London: British Library, 1986.

———. "Speech-Manuscript-Print." In *New Directions in Textual Studies.* Edited by David Oliphant and Robin Bradford. Austin: Harry Ransom Humanities Research Center, 1990. 86–89. Reprinted in McKenzie, *Making Meaning: "Printers of the Mind" and Other Essays.* Edited by Peter D. McDonald and Michael F. Suarez. Amherst, Mass.: Universit y of Massachusetts Press, 2002. 237–58.

McLuhan, Marshall. *The Gutenberg Galaxy: The Making of Typographic Man.* Toronto: University of Toronto Press, 1962.

Marin, Louis. *Portrait of the King.* Translated by Martha Houle. Minneapolis: University of Minnesota Press, 1988.

Martín Abad, Julián. *La imprenta en Alcalá de Henares (1502–1600).* Madrid: Arco Libros, 1991. 3 vols.

Martínez de Bujanda, Jesús., ed. *Index des livres interdits.* Geneva: Droz, 1984–1996. 10 vols.

Moll, Jaime. *De la imprenta al lector: Estudios sobre el libro español de los siglos XVI al XVII.* Instrumenta Bibliológica. Madrid: Arco Libros, 1994.

Moreno Gallego, Valentín. "*Nescit vox missa reverti*: cuatro palabras sobre el control de la escritura en la modernidad española." In *La investigación y las fuentes documentales de los archivos.* Cuadernos de Archivos y Bibliotecas de Castilla-La Mancha 3, vol. 2. Guadalajara: Anabad Castilla-La Mancha, Asociación de Amigos del Archivo Histórico Provincial, 1996. 2 vols. 1155–74.

Moss, Ann. *Printed Commonplace-Books and the Structuring of Renaissance Thought.* Oxford: Clarendon Press, 1996.

Muto, Giovanni. "Classificazioni e generi: dai libri di Gobierno y Estado ai Livres Politiques." In *El libro antiguo español IV: Coleccionismo y bibliotecas (siglos XV–XVII).* Edited by María Luisa López-Vidriero, Pedro M. Cátedra, and María Isabel Hernández González. Salamanca: Universidad de Salamanca, 1998. 505–17.

Nalle, Sara T. *God in La Mancha: Religious Reform and the People of Cuenca, 1500–1650.* Baltimore: John Hopkins University Press, 1992.

Ong, Walter. *Orality and Literacy: The Technologizing of the Word.* London: Routledge, 1982.

Palomo, Federico. *"Disciplina christiana.* Apuntes historiográficos en torno a la disciplina y el disciplinamiento social como categorías de la historia religiosa de la alta Edad Moderna." *Cuadernos de Historia Moderna* 18 (1997): 119–36.

Pardo Tomás, José. *Ciencia y censura: La inquisición española y los libros científicos en los siglos XVI y XVII.* Madrid: Consejo Superior de Investigaciones Científicas, 1991.

Paredes Alonso, Javier. *Mercaderes de libros: Cuatro siglos de historia de la Hermandad de san Gerónimo.* Madrid: Fundación Germán Sánchez Ruipérez, 1988.

Pedraza García, Manuel José. *La producción y distribución del libro en Zaragoza, 1501–1521.* Saragossa: Institución Fernando el Católico, 1997.

Peña Díaz, Manuel. *Cataluña en el Renacimiento: libros y lenguas, Barcelona, 1473–1600.* Lleida: Milenio, 1996.

———. *El laberinto de los libros: Historia cultural de la Barcelona del Quinientos.* Madrid: Pirámide, 1997.

Petrucci, Armando, ed. *Libri, editori e pubblico nell'Europa moderna: Guida storica e critica.* Rome: Laterza, 1977.

———. *Public Lettering: Script, Power, and Culture.* Chicago: University of Chicago Press, 1993.

———, ed. *La scrittura: Ideologia e rappresentazione.* Turin: Einaudi, 1987.

———. *Writers and Readers in Medieval Italy: Studies in the History of Written Culture.* New Haven, Conn.: Yale University Press, 1995.

———. *Writing the Dead: Death and Writing Strategies in the Western Tradition.* Stanford, Calif.: Stanford University Press, 1998.

Pinto Crespo, Virgilio. *Inquisición y control ideológico en la España del siglo XVI.* La Otra Historia de España 9. Madrid: Taurus, 1983.

Portús, Javier and Jesusa Vega. *La estampa religiosa en la España del Antiguo Régimen.* Publicaciones de la Fundación Universitaria Española, Bellas Artes 12. Madrid: Fundación Universitaria Española, 1998.

Prieto Bernabé, J. M. "Lectura y lectores en el Madrid de los Austrias. 1550–1650." Dissertation, Universidad Complutense de Madrid, 1998.

Rocha, Andrée Crabbé. *A epistolografía em Portugal.* Lisbon: Imprensa Nacional-Casa da Moeda, 1985.

Rodríguez de Diego, José Luis. "La formación del Archivo de Simancas en el siglo XVI. Función y orden interno." In *El libro antiguo español, IV. Coleccionismo y bibliotecas (siglos XV–XVII).* Edited by María Luisa López-Vidriero, Pedro M. Cátedra, and María Isabel Hernández González. Salamanca: Universidad de Salamanca, 1998. 519–57.

Rojo Vega, Anastasio. *Impresores, libreros y papeleros en Medina del Campo y Valladolid en el siglo XVII.* Valladolid: Junta de Castilla y León, Consejería de Cultura y Turismo, 1994.

Romano, Giovanni. "Usi religiosi e produzione figurativa nel Cinquecento:

qualche sintomo di crisi." In *Libri, idee e sentimienti nel Cinquecento italiano*. Edited by A. Prosperi and A. Bioni. Modena: Panini, 1987. 155–63.

Rossi, Pietro, ed. *La memoria del sapere: Forme di conservazione e strutture organizzative dall'Antichità a oggi*. Rome: Laterza, 1988.

Rueda Ramírez, Pedro. "La circulación de libros entre el viejo y el nuevo mundo en la Sevilla de finales del siglo XVI y comienzos del XVII." *Cuadernos de Historia Moderna* 22 (1999): 79–105.

Sánchez Mariana, Manuel. *Bibliófilos españoles: Desde sus orígenes hasta los albores del siglo XX*. Madrid: Biblioteca Nacional, 1993.

Serrera, Juan Miguel. "Alonso Sánchez Coello y la mecánica del retrato de corte." In *Alonso Sánchez Coello y el retrato en la corte de Felipe II*. Edited by Santiago Saavedra. Madrid: Museo del Prado, 1990. 37–63.

Spufford, Margaret. *Small Books and Pleasant Histories: Popular Fiction and Its Readership in Seventeenth-Century England*. London: Methuen, 1981.

Testón Núñez, Isabel, Rocío Sánchez Rubio, and María Angeles Hernández Bermejo. *El buscador de gloria: Guerra y magia en la vida de un hidalgo castellano del siglo XVI*. Alcalá de Henares: Centro de Estudios Cervantinos, 1998.

Thorton, Dora. *The Scholar in his Study: Ownership and Experience in Renaissance Italy*. New Haven: Yale University Press, 1998.

Torremocha, Margarita. *La vida estudiantil en el Antiguo Régimen*. Madrid: Alianza, 1998.

Varela, Julia. *Modos de educación en la España de la Contrarreforma*. Genealogía del Poder 9. Madrid: La Piqueta, 1983.

Verrier, Frédérique. *Les armes de Minerve: L'humanisme militaire dans l'Italie du XVIe siècle*. Paris: Presses de l'Université de Paris-Sorbonne, 1997.

Viñao Fraga, Antonio. "Alfabetización, lectura y escritura en el Antiguo Régimen (siglos XVI–XVII)." In *Leer y escribir en España: Doscientos años de alfabetización*. Edited by Agustín Escolano. Madrid: Pirámide, 1992. 45–68.

Watt, Tessa. *Cheap Print and Popular Piety, 1550–1640*. Cambridge: Cambridge University Press, 1991.

Woudhuysen, H. R. *Sir Philip Sidney and the Circulation of Manuscripts, 1558–1640*. Oxford: Clarendon Press, 1996.

Yates, Frances A. *The Art of Memory*. Chicago: University of Chicago Press, 1966.

Index of Names

Acknowledgments

The first part of this little book includes the lectures for the graduate seminar "Reading in the Golden Age," I taught while a visiting professor in the Department of Hispanic and Italian Studies at Johns Hopkins University in November and December 1998. Because of the book's inception as lectures, the bibliography and notes are therefore simple, and the presentation of issues and lines of research serves more as a synthesis than as an exhaustive monograph. Nevertheless, despite its necessary concision, the material base of this synthesis has been constructed with first-hand documentary sources. I hope my references to these sources here will draw attention to the possibility—nay, the necessity—of building a history of the book and written culture by turning to uncustomary but fundamental sources and by reexamining from an uncustomary point of view those sources that are familiar. I have attempted to outline a history of communication during the Spanish Golden Age that would bring together speech, images and written texts, presenting them as all serving the same objective: the will to know and to create memory.

Although this is a brief book, the list of acknowledgments is long. First, I must recognize the group of students for whom these pages were originally intended, and also Professor Harry Sieber, who generously made possible my presence at Johns Hopkins. During those months, Claudia Sieber posed the sharpest and most challenging questions I have ever faced. Roger Chartier's teachings should be evident in several passages, unless my own ineptness has spoiled his good efforts. The collaboration of my colleagues in the task force on

"Information and Communication," part of the European Science Foundation's project, "Cultural Exchange in Europe, ca. 1400–1700," led me to better understand the advantages of a multifaceted approach to cultural analysis. The colloquia and seminars at the University of Salamanca's Seminary on Medieval and Renaissance Studies have allowed me to discuss and improve upon some of the ideas presented here. My sincerest thanks to its members. The tutelary genius of Pedro M. Cátedra, always generous, beneficent, and kind, has helped round out this text in its final shape.

Madrid, November 1999

www.ingramcontent.com/pod-product-compliance
Lightning Source LLC
Chambersburg PA
CBHW030356100426
42812CB00028B/2733/J